Caring for Your Older **DOG**

also by Kathleen Berman and Bill Landesman
How to Train Your Dog in Six Weeks

Caring for Your Older DOG

Kathleen Berman and Bill Landesman

ARCO PUBLISHING, INC.
NEW YORK

First Arco Edition

Published by Arco Publishing, Inc.
215 Park Avenue South, New York, N.Y. 10003

Copyright © 1984, 1978 by Kathleen Berman and Bill Landesman
Originally published by Frederick Fell Publishers, Inc.

Library of Congress Cataloging in Publication Data

Berman, Kathleen.
  Caring for your older dog.

  Reprint. Originally published: How to care for your
older dog / Bill Landesman and Kathleen Berman. New York:
F. Fell Publishers, c1978.
  1. Dogs. 2. Dogs—Diseases. 3. Veterinary geriatrics.
I. Landesman, Bill. II. Title.
SF427.B5177 1984   636.7'089897   84-2861
ISBN 0-668-06082-4 (pbk.)

Printed in the United States of America

ACKNOWLEDGMENTS

This book is dedicated with much love to our own adorable pets, DREAM, FLIRT, POOH CAT, OPIELINE, RALPHIE BOY, FLUFFY, E.T., TEDDIE GIRL, LITTLE FELLA, RINGY, HAPPIE, CHARLSIE, SENNA, LOVEY, BUTTER FLUTTER, SNOW WHITE, PRINCE, SIMONE, and GARFINCKLE. Our wonderful menagerie provides us with countless hours of joy, amusement, fascination, and challenge. Communication between mankind and his animal friends is assuredly one of life's most precious gifts.

Special memory to our German Shepherd, FRITZ, who will always live in that special place in our hearts.

Our deepest gratitude to Karen and Chuck, whose encouragement and belief in us considerably enriched this venture.

We wish to thank our charming model, Karen Landesman, for lending an irresistible appeal to the animal photos.

Again, we wish to acknowledge the expertise of our photographer, Charles Berman, who did a masterful job of capturing detail with great clarity, and who used humor and great imagination overall.

CONTENTS

FOREWORD

This book is about the older dog. It was written to fill a tremendous gap in literature pertaining to our pets and their advanced years. It is surprising how little has been devoted to the aging process in animals; but, then, many people do not like to think about the concept of aging or its attendant social implications either in themselves or in their pets. Society idolizes youth and seemingly turns it back on age. Senior citizenship in dogs and in people produces a social stigma; as the years pile up, the individual discovers feelings of shame or guilt for having had the audacity to grow old!

Unfortunately, these ideas pervade our rational thoughts and allow us to pass some of this irrational guilt on to our older dogs. Dogs are extremely perceptive to love and genuine concern, but also to rejection. They act as receptors to all the feelings you as an individual engender in yourself and pass on to others.

The person who is growing older along with his or her dog can often empathize with the aging process in his pet. The health of the relationship between the older person and the older dog depends in large part upon the wholesomeness of the person's attitude toward aging. If an owner embraces a somewhat pragmatic philosophy, he or she will convey this attitude to the dog. In turn, the older dog will feel a comfortable self-respect, free from the shackles of bigotry and social stigma.

If you view aging as an experience that is neither to be ashamed of nor denied, then you understand that age can bring with it a new dignity, mellowness, and wisdom. You will also understand that age is an irrevocable evolution of the seasons, something to face with charity and compassion, as well as gratitude for the composite experiences of life.

This concept is very relevant to the older dog. It is paramount in recognizing aging as an inseparable component of living and must be understood before one is able to experience the proper reverence for life itself. THE QUALITY OF LIFE IS INDISPUTABLY MORE IMPORTANT THAN ITS MERE LONGEVITY. This realization is most important. It helps us to appreciate and celebrate each new day with our beloved pet throughout all the seasons of his life.

What do we mean by "older" when referring to our dogs? Aging can occur more rapidly in certain dogs. The giant breeds such as Great Danes, Irish Wolfhounds, and St. Bernards are noted for their short life spans. These breeds are old at some eight years, whereas a Toy Poodle, Maltese, or Shih Tzu may not be considered old until the age of twelve or fourteen years. Generally speaking, it seems predictable that the smaller the dog, the longer the life span; the larger the dog, the shorter the life span. When a dog suffers an incurable debility at a chronologically youthful age, he can still be regarded as old in a biological sense—his body is not renewing its cells with sufficient rapidity to insure his survival. An animal may have a genetic predisposition to some chronic malfunction or degenerative disease that will cause him to age before his time. He becomes a "little old man" far more rapidly than his healthy counterpart. Thus, heredity is a large factor in aging. Consideration and compassion should be just as great for the young "older" dog as for the family pet who lives out his normal life span.

Most people don't understand what aging is or why it occurs. In brief, the body is composed of millions of cells of myriad types, corresponding to all the different organs and tissues in the body. Throughout the lifetime of the organism, be it human or canine, these cells enjoy a constant replacement; they are nourished by valuable nutrients transported to them through the bloodstream. The bloodstream carries life-giving oxygen and nutrients to the cells, and takes away toxic waste matter. Cells die, but are replenished by new ones. In turn, these cells live out their life span and are subsequently replaced by another new complex of cells. An organism receives a new complement of cells about every eleven months. The aging process becomes apparent when the cells of the body die off faster than they can be replaced. So, it becomes expedient for us first to consider what happens in aging, and then for us to try to arrest the aging process by ensuring a healthy replacement of new cells for old.

Can one alter the course of aging? The power is within our grasp and seems so simple that it is often overlooked. The key to prolonging the life process lies in proper nutrition and a proper mental attitude. *Caring for Your Older Dog* will deal extensively with preventive nutrition for dogs of any age, culminating with the older dog. Awareness of proper nutrition is one of the most meaningful aspects of dealing with the infirmities of old age. You will begin to realize that, as Hippocrates stated, "Food Shall Be Your Medicine and Medicine Your Food." So be it with you and your older dog.

Many owners harbor a fear that the older dog will inevitably be felled by some disastrous infirmity. This is not true. Most dogs advance into old age with little or no perceptible change in their health. Old age is *not* a disease, nor must it be accompanied by disease. Dogs are not psychologically devastated by age unless it brings with it some very painful infirmities. In the aging process the body normally experiences only a decline in activity, a lessening of energy, and a reduction in the efficiency of organs and glands.

In this age of uncertainty people are looking to the reliable companionship of the dog. His noble and undemanding nature makes him a treasured friend to many lonely people who have no other form of companionship. As your dog advances in years, the bond becomes stronger. I consider myself a pragmatic person. I believe in the importance of "now," and feel that a person should celebrate every day as though no others were forthcoming. In this way, each of us activates his inner glow and offers this warmth to all of those in the circle of his affections. When life's fires are snuffed out, one cannot retrospectively examine the fullness of his life, nor have regrets for kindnesses left undone. The older dog doesn't think about a past or plan for the future. He is not fearful of death for he does not comprehend it in human terms. He is aware only of the "now" in his life. The older dog does not meditate bitterly on such matters as death and infirmity. He makes the most of every day. We humans can learn from this.

Hopefully, this book will answer a myriad of questions you have waiting. In addressing the subject of the older dog, with all its ramifications, we hope we have included all you will need to know to become a better friend, companion, and, when necessary, nurse. We will discuss personality and habit changes in the older dog, the handicapped dog, general health care, the diseases of aging, basic nutrition, preventive medicine at any age, obedience and the older dog, causes of death, coping with death, and, finally, the new puppy. We will have come full circle, taking into consideration all of your dog's needs along the way.

Our book is intended to offer you the voluminous information that can reasonably be put into practice *before* your dog has a chance to suffer the many preventable afflictions of old age, as well as information that will make the already-afflicted older dog comfortable and easy in his declining years. It is not how old we are chronologically that matters, but how old we think, feel, and act. Life is meant to be lived, not tolerated. You must tell yourself that all things are possible. And, in the case of your older dog, all things you are capable of giving in goodness and love are very worthwhile.

This book can help to improve the quality of your pet's life. You don't have to wait until your dog is older to read it.

Kathleen Berman and Bill Landesman

Caring for Your Older DOG

Bill Landesman's "Dream the Wonder Poodle" recalls and carries over a high jump. Dream is a national television star and one of the few attack-trained poodles in the country.

Chapter I

PERSONALITY AND HABIT
CHANGES IN THE OLDER DOG

The Aging Dog

People who relate to their dogs as to another person will have the most difficult task adjusting to the dog aging. These people cherish the devotion, predictability, and companionship in a manner so committed that they fear never being able to withstand the death of their animal. Some people have put themselves into an early grave grieving over the loss of a dog, just as some dogs decline rapidly after the demise of their masters. It is not for any of us to pass judgment upon the degree of commitment one should feel for his or her dog.

On the other side of the coin, we have people who fancy themselves pragmatic who will allow a blemish on the dog's skin to blossom into a golf-ball-size tumor without ever thinking of calling the vet. They reason that if it was meant to disappear, it would, and if it was meant to be fatal, there is nothing they could do anyhow. This sort of reasoning is not pragmatism but capricious folly. When your dog is young, you afford him the concern of calling the vet should changes occur in behavior, bowel habits, eating habits, or in any unfamiliar phenomena. With the older dog, you must be ever more watchful of subtle changes that could require attention. Death is not inevitable at a certain age. You can significantly forestall the ravages of time by being more attentive to your dog's needs and by acting quickly when you suspect something to be amiss.

The Need For Attention

The older dog is in many senses a big baby. As much as he basked in affection when he was younger, he will require even more

1

as he gets older. Your dog is not quite as sure of himself now. His world is closing in on him, getting smaller. He is not that actively involved in the comings and goings of the outside world. He is losing interest in other dogs from the standpoints of playfulness, sexuality, and aggression. The fight syndrome declines with age, as do adventures with the opposite sex. The older dog simply doesn't have the energy, alertness, stamina, speed, or agility for all these previously savored shenanigans. Now, you and the immediate family are actually his entire world! He looks to that world for comfort, support, and love. Your dog was never just an animated fixture in the house, and now more than ever, you should be more intent on setting aside some time to pat him gently and communicate with him softly. Other members of the household should be instructed to do the same so long as they don't make pests of themselves. If certain members are too young to comprehend this difference then it is better they stay at a safe distance.

Irritability

An older dog with failing health and accompanying medical problems finds himself a little sensitive or grouchy about things that may not ordinarily have bothered him in the past. When your dog was younger, he may never have minded someone accidently walking or bumping into him while he was resting or sleeping on the floor. In his prime he was able to tolerate it when you took away his food bowl while he was eating, to add a few more tidbits. He graciously allowed himself to be physically pestered by an infant or small child who either didn't know any better or who had not been instructed in proper consideration for the family pet. Your older dog even romped with joy when playing with the family cat or with another dog in the family who was most likely much younger than he. But now, any of these trifles appear to him to be very great annoyances.

The discomfort your older dog may feel is magnified by his failing senses, senses which may no longer warn him of an impending approach by man or beast. His impaired senses may be giving him no warning to avoid, or at least be mentally prepared for, shocks. This can make any confrontation a startlingly frightful experience for him. Because of possible stomach trouble, hip trouble, kidney problems, or other infirmities that often accompany the aging process, there can also be a very real increase in pain. Your older dog may also on occasion, be growling a bit whereas he never did before. This new behavior could anger you; you may want to hit or reprimand him in

2

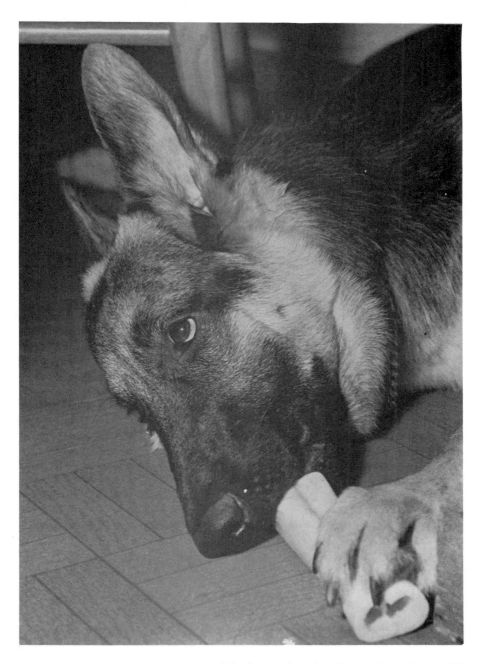

Now that your dog is older, you and the immediate family are his entire world. He looks to that world for comfort, support, and love.

YOUR "OLD" DOG MAY BE LESS TOLERANT OF THINGS HE USED TO PUT UP WITH GLADLY.

some way. It would be unfortunate to act upon this initial impulse, for you must first understand the probable causes of such a newly manifested crotchety attitude on the part of your older dog.

Many unpleasant incidents can be completely avoided if a little forethought is used. Wait until your dog is finished eating the food in his bowl before picking it up to refill it; this eliminates any possible hostility or anxieties from cropping up. Such consideration on your part will even bring you an admiring "thank you" glance when you refill the bowl and return it to him. Likewise, using care not to walk into your dog is certainly not too much of a price to pay for the many happy years he has shared with you.

Eating

What are some other subtle signs of aging? Your dog will become

4

Dogs should eat out of heavy bowls so they don't have to chase their food across the floor.

less interested in household activities, less ebullient, less apt to run to the door when the bell rings, less hungry, more thirsty; he will require more sleep and more frequent trips to relieve himself. He will also require more frequent, but smaller meals of higher-quality or higher-biological-value protein. His coat will begin to thin out. It will become dryer and less luxuriant. Your dog will shed less. With the change in his inclination toward food, and the slowing down of his metabolism, he can maintain his weight. But if you get into the habit of coaxing and seducing the older dog into eating more, from a fear that he is not eating enough, then you will cause him to become neurotic about food, becoming a poor eater or perhaps gaining excess weight. *In gaining weight, he will also be shortening his natural life span.*

Exercise

Old age brings with it a certain stiffness in the joints. Older dogs will be slower to walk, slower to rise, and slower to lie down; all

5

movement is much more of an effort. Discouraging exercise completely, however, would be to deny the body's ability to regenerate itself through exercise. If you live in a walk-up apartment and your dog is slowing down, but is not in excruciating pain, encourage him to walk up and down the stairs. Most dogs, young and old, don't get enough exercise anyway. Exercise is an aerobic activity that brings oxygen and nutrients to cells all over the body, depending of course on what areas are worked. Anything that brings oxygen to the cells brings with it the vital life force to regenerate the cells. Encourage your old dog to exercise moderately but consistently. You will be increasing his life span.

Sexuality

As your older dog will be less inclined toward vigorous exercise, he or she will also likely feel less attraction for copulating with the opposite sex. This does not hold true for all dogs, however, since females essentially remain fertile till death, although they come into heat less frequently with age. But because a female can conceive is no reason to allow her this draining experience at an old age. It may very well kill her. Males also may remain potent till death, but the testicles begin to shrink with age and the seminal fluid is less virile. Copulation for an older male can also signal his death; some older dogs have a sexual fervor that goes beyond the realm of common sense. In general, a male or female beyond the age of seven or eight, should not be encouraged in sexual matters.

Incontinence

Another common problem with older dogs is incontinence, meaning the inability to hold urine. Your dog will need to be walked more frequently. If control regresses, then you would do well to consider a housebreaking routine, as used for puppies. The schedule is described later; in Chapter IX). But, should the problem of dribbling his urine around the house become a daily occurrence, and if all else fails because of extreme medical conditions, a humane alternative is to partially paper-train him. Since it is unreasonable to reprimand him for actions beyond his control, provide a papered area in the kitchen, bathroom, or basement. Providing papers for the dog who suffers incontinence in no way eliminates the housebreaking routine. It simply augments the housebreaking, making life with and for the older dog more enjoyable.

Jealousy

The older dog may tend toward more possessiveness of family and physical possessions. He is less favorably disposed toward sharing people and things. As he gets older, his need for more affection, coupled with his increasing insecurity, can add up to increased jealousy. If he wasn't jealous before of the affection family members display for each other, then he is less likely to feel jealousy just because he is older. If he has always had a tendency toward jealous display in his youth, then the aging process will only serve to make it worse. For the jealous dog, make sure you show him ample affection, and don't flaunt affection for members of the family in front of him if this seems to disturb him. If someone in the family has the idea of introducing a bouncy new puppy into the household, either to cheer up the older dog or to cushion his imminent demise, you should consider very carefully the possible consequences of such a seemingly innocent move.

Don't count on cheering up the older dog, whose strong instinct at this point is to obtain all the affection for himself. The older dog can display overt jealousy toward a new pup, injuring or even killing it. Even if the jealousy is suppressed by the older dog, this internalization will lead to his own illness. That is not to say that a young addition to the family inevitably leads to an unfortunate outcome. We have seen and heard of young pups who have given an older dog a new lease on life. They provide companionship, and induce the old dog to feel and act younger. But for as many happy endings as we have seen, there can be twice that number of sheer disasters. When the new addition doesn't work out, damage is inflicted upon the younger dog also. Jealousy and intimidation from the older dog can make the pup fearful and shy; the pup could develop into a fear-biter. Either way you crack it, this is one tough nut. One should be wary of such possibilities with an older dog, regardless of urgings from family or friends.

Senility

The older dog does not become senile in the human sense. He is just as intelligent as he was in his prime. Because his actions are slower, we should not assume that his wits are too. In terms of human senility, people have an inclination to drift off into a fantasy world and lose contact with reality. Dogs' senses are dulled, but they don't suffer the confusion and disorientation associated with senility in humans.

7

Kenneling

If your older dog is used to vacationing away from home at kennels, then it will not be a traumatic event for him to visit a kennel as he grows older. However, all kennels and their respective attendants cannot be relied upon to treat your dog with the extra consideration he requires now. An experience that was tolerable in his youth can become most disturbing when he is older. Also, any time you board your dog at a kennel or at the vet's, you are risking his health. Close proximity to many other dogs, sick or otherwise, increases the risk of disease. Your dog is more vulnerable at his age. So if you don't have to expose him to kennel life, no matter how brief the stay, don't do it. If your older dog is not familiar with the kennel experience, then it could be an experience that will so unnerve him that it could cost you his life. Your dog can view the alien kennel environment as abandonment. He has no way of relating to time. As far as he is concerned, you have left him and are never coming back. The best way to accommodate the necessary travel is to have someone stay with the dog in his own familiar surroundings. If this someone is familiar to the dog, so much the better. Next best would be to have someone familiar take the dog to his or her house or apartment. If the dog is going to be moved to another location, and the person taking him is not familiar to him, then, if at all possible, have that person stay with the dog for a day or two at your house before taking him away. Otherwise, the experience for the older dog can well be as traumatic as being boarded out at a kennel. Never take an older dog with you on a plane unless absolutely necessary. The trip in the baggage compartment could disorient him enough to make him terminally ill.

Being Left Alone at Home

The older dog will be quite comfortable being left alone if this is a normal course of events for him. Should the household consist of a working couple, there is no reason to assume that one or both of them should stay home just to keep the old boy company. Dogs are comfortable with what is familiar. If the old dog is used to people being around him all the time, it may be a more difficult adjustment to make a radical change in his household activities. It is preferable not to suddenly leave the older dog alone for long periods of time. Outside of the insecurity it could foster, it will doubtless make a change in his housebreaking schedule also.

The older dog should be walked more often, not less. If your dog has to be left alone for long periods of time, whether he is used to it or not, you should provide for his frequent relief by having someone come in and walk him at midday, when possible. This is important if you are going to be gone on a regular basis for nine hours or more. Don't expect your older dog to be a hero. Provide for his changing needs.

Barking

Should the household where someone was home all day become one where the dog is left alone for long periods of time, the older dog may become more anxiety-ridden and show it through barking. However, if the family maintains its long-standing schedule of activity, there is no reason to expect increased barking from an older dog. But if radical changes in the comings and goings of the family are necessary and the older dog shows insecurity by barking excessively, he can very often be soothed by soft music when you leave, to drown out outside noises, and by plenty of interesting and tasty chew-toys to play with, handed to him as you leave. Very often, enlarging the area in which you keep him will give him more breathing space, and less chance of becoming bored or feeling shut in.

Graying

Graying can be a sign of aging, but it by no means always accompanies old age. Many dogs gray prematurely, as do people. This is in part due to insufficient PABA in the diet. PABA is para-aminobenzoic acid, one of the B vitamins. If you have a prematurely graying dog, you may want to look into the possibility of supplementing his diet with PABA. Gray hair is hair that has lost its color pigmentation—don't judge a dog as being over the hill on the basis alone of his gray hair or the absence of it.

Estimating Age

Some people estimate a dog's age to be equivalent to seven years for every one year of a human's life. Other authorities claim that this is not so. They evaluate the dog's first year as being equivalent to the first twenty-one years of human life. After the first year, they add four for every dog-year lived. By the first method, a dog at the age of ten, will be the human equivalent of seventy years. Figured the second way, a dog at ten years will be the human equivalent of fifty-seven ($9 \times 4 = 36$, plus 21). We cannot be sure that we can equate dog years in human terms, or even that we should. We know how long the average dog lives, and we also know that we can increase that

YOUR "OLD" DOG MAY CONTINUE TO SURPRISE YOU WITH FEATS OF STRENGTH AND ENDURANCE.

average through genetics, nutrition, and psychological factors. Perhaps these areas are what we'd best concentrate on.

Genetic factors play a prominent role in the aging process since genetic heritage is unique and unchanging. Awareness of this, however, should never be a reason for you not to allow your dog to realize his full genetic potential.

Children in the House

To children, dogs are fun as long as they can romp tirelessly and play fetch with a favorite stick or ball. They allow themselves to be fondled till the little people find something better to do; they don't have to go to the potty too often and don't require feeding too often; they don't mind being wakened from a sound, restful sleep when the children tramp in from school and stumble over the good fellow en masse, cascading books and papers on him and around where he was lying so peacefully.

The aging process in the family pet is not often attended by an acute awareness on the part of the small children. Very often these playmates view the aging dog as essentially the same vivacious playmate he was several years before. It is usually the older dog who must give a very definitive indication as to the physical and psychological changes that have taken place. The older dog will often become more impatient with roughhousing, shorter on energy, less adept at getting around, less able to see clearly, less proficient at assimilating food, more inclined to sleep long hours, more inclined toward accidents in the house, less delighted with elaborate jaunts around the neighborhood, and more inclined to snappy behavior. None of these should be surprising since we can also relate most of these characteristics to the older person.

We don't mean to imply that all children are insensitive to the changing needs of the older dog. But many more than you would think are totally insensitive to the basic rules of etiquette and decency even around the young healthy dog, and this condition has to become exacerbated in the case of the older dog. If you asked a number of children which they would rather relinquish, their family dog or the TV set, you might be shocked at the collective responses.

The first place to try to effect a positive change in attitude would be with the parents. Sensitive, loving mothers and fathers breed and nurture sensitive, loving little people. The ideal situation would definitely not be ruled by tyranny—"If you don't take Rex out for his extra walk this afternoon, you will not be allowed to watch television tonight." To pit a young child's sense of responsibility against his manic need for television is dastardly business indeed. The child will most certainly resent the association, and the older dog will become discomforted by the child's indicated antagonism. If you fail to rally the children's responsibility for the dog with a sense of temperance and charity, then it is far better for the older dog that the children relinquish their grudging duties and leave them to a family member who is more loving and responsive. This release from responsibility is not the best thing for developing character in the growing child, but if his or her activities with the older dog are constantly involved in conflict, it will most certainly affect the health and life span of your older dog adversely. The family's commitment to the older dog should be in keeping with a commitment one would make to the grandparents in a household. Devotion should not be meted out to the tune of so many dollars, or so many hours. I feel that one need never be ashamed of doing too much. If you must err, do so on the side of being more loving and responsive to your aging pet.

Emotions and Illness

As children are small people with a full spectrum of emotions

Love between children and animals is a beautiful experience for all.

12

and feelings that need to be acknowledged, in the same way, we must not be blind to the nuances and potency of a dog's emotions. When we mistreat them, they suffer psychological damage. As the unhappy child will manifest clinical diseases that would not have occurred if the child felt cared for, wanted, loved, so the dog who is unhappy because of mistreatment will become ill and age prematurely. This is not to suggest that you become a totally permissive parent and allow your dog to run amuck. But it does mean that you must consider the very real physical damage that emotional turmoil can bring to your older dog.

Treat your dog with the same sense of compassion and decency you should reserve for your children. A tortured mind can bring destruction to a healthy body. Conversely, a healthy mind can be tainted by a diseased body. Never discount the power of the mind to heal or to harm. Keep your older dog happy, and he will surely reflect this concern with a healthier and longer life!

Children can learn to be very responsible and gentle in caring for a dog.

Kathy Berman with her pet squirrel, E.T. "EeTee" was found on the lawn at one day old and reared on a totally natural diet of nuts, seeds, sprouts, fruits, and vegetables. He is now one year old. A healthful diet is essential for all living creatures.

Even pros have to take a break sometime!

Chapter II

THE HANDICAPPED DOG

Handicaps are not the exclusive domain of the older dog, but a handicap can make a dog appear and act older than his years. It can also affect him adversely psychologically, so that, in fact, he will age prematurely. Don't be too quick to view a mild infirmity as a handicap. You will be surprised at how much a positive attitude can rebuild health and confidence in many a disabled dog.

A handicap, by definition, is some infirmity or disability that can impair the normal average functioning of an animal. A handicap also suggests an impairment that has been or will be malfunctioning over a lengthy period of time. It does not suggest an acute physical ailment from which there is a quick recovery. Many handicaps are the direct result of degenerative ailments such as kidney malfunction, diabetes, progressive blindness, gradual hearing loss, arthritis, slipped discs, cancer, heart and lung problems, prostate enlargements, and incontinence. These dysfunctions and many more can truly handicap a dog's potential for maximum enjoyment of life, will impair his mobility and self-confidence, and can lead to a depression that could cause a willful premature death. An animal who requires constant attention or consideration, over and above the norm for an older dog, may be considered handicapped. How his owners and family view his impairments will decide largely how well he accepts his fate. It also indicates how handicapped the owners themselves really are both in the mental and physical senses.

17

Accidents

There is another category by which the dog, irrespective of age, may become handicapped. This is the acute (sudden) handicap that is not gradual (chronic) or degenerative in origin. Such handicap is the direct result of an auto accident or other sudden mishap. Accidents are all too common with pets, and much more frighteningly common than most people would realize. The average person is usually only aware of the happenings within his own immediate range of activities. Professionals who work in animal clinics have a different perspective. The halls of these hospitals are crowded with victims of assorted mishaps.

One of the most preventable types of accident, and yet one of the most frequent, is being struck by an automobile. The role of the automobile in the handicapping of dogs is acknowledged: cars are the number-one killer of both dogs and cats. The toll of the automobile is far and above that of any natural, degenerative disease, and dogs that are not killed outright by cars are very often maimed for life, so that, depending upon the extent of debility, death may be preferable to a serious handicap. *People are at the core of responsibility.* It is safe to say that cars, and the irresponsibility of people, bear the blame for more handicaps of an acute nature than all degenerative diseases combined. It is the driver who can ensure or deny the safety of a dog. The assumption of greater human responsibility will result in far fewer dead dogs and far fewer handicapped dogs.

Yet it is not primarily the uncaring, or even the hapless motorist that can be charged as an executioner. The ultimate accountability for a dog's safety lies with its owner. The paramount precaution we can take against a dead or handicapped dog is that common, everyday item—the leash. People who allow their animals to walk themselves will eventually suffer the backlash of this misplaced liberality. Those who question the validity of what we say should seek out their own family vet, and ask him or her for an unbiased opinion on the gravity of the situation.

Mutual Adjustments

When your dog has become handicapped, try to assess objectively his attitude toward his infirmity. Each individual dog handles his infirmities differently from the next. Do not credit your dog with feelings he does not possess. Do not grieve for his fate. If a handicapped dog is not in excruciating pain, he, in all probability, will ac-

18

cept his fate with very good humor. Remember that dogs do not plan for the future nor do they bemoan an unfulfilled past. Dogs relate only to the immediacy of the *now* in their lives. To achieve the maximum relationship with your handicapped dog, don't exaggerate your pity for him or for yourself.

Loss of a Limb

As the result of an auto accident, the loss of a limb is fairly common. Most people would think a dog could not survive with a missing limb. Far fewer people would imagine that the dog could actually thrive, feeling essentially no debility whatever, except for tiring a bit more quickly when walking. One missing limb is quite workable for the average dog, be it front or rear. Two or more missing limbs become another question, with a much less favorable prognosis. A dog with three legs can walk, run, or pull you down the street just as exuberantly as he can on all fours. This is not to recommend that you allow your dog to run amuck just because he is disabled.

On the contrary, there is a tendency to be all too accomodating to his sometimes unreasonable demands. So, just as obedience training, with certain modifications, can be accomplished at any age, so can obedience training be instituted with the three-legged dog, or with almost any handicapped dog, be the handicap loss of sight, hearing, limb, or whatever. In fact, obedience training is one of the most positive things you can do for your handicapped dog. It will serve to strengthen him physically, as well as to build his confidence emotionally.

This comment may smack of brazen callousness to some. But obedience training actually does serve as rehabilitation in its most positive sense. Obedience sets certain behavioral guidelines that allow both you and the dog a more constructive relationship. A certain degree of forced exercise, via obedience training, can serve to strengthen the three remaining limbs, and especially the one that has to assume all the weight in the front or rear. You want the dog to develop compensatory strength, otherwise he may become habitually lazy, avoiding the urge to relieve himself when necessary. This in turn can lead to faulty elimination, constipation problems, the storage of excess uremic waste, and, with these, a whole host of other degenerative diseases. Then the dog will develop degenerative handicaps to add to the physical ones.

19

Spinal Damage

Very often a dog will suffer spinal damage from degenerative processes. This is usually referred to as "slipped discs," but they are not really discs at all, and they have not really slipped. Essentially what has occurred is a loss of resiliency between the vertebrae, and so-called slipped disc can be the result of an accident or, more likely, a gradual degenerative progression that shows itself in one of the body's weakened areas. A contributory factor could be lack of exercise (a sedentary life-style in which the older dog very frequently indulges). Lack of exercise decreases blood flow to vital areas, slackening the muscles and allowing the intervertebral "shock absorbers" to become thinner and less resilient, thereby leading to possible perforation upon impact. Diet is also a factor, since the cells that make up the "shock absorbers" are being starved for nutrients, which impairs their vitality and regenerative ability.

Whether the origin lies in degeneration from lack of exercise and poor nutrition, or the slipped disc results from an auto accident or other acute calamity, rehabilitative factors remain the same. The dog needs to be put on an optimum diet containing ample amounts of vitamin C and its complex, the bioflavonoids, which are also classified as vitamin P. The dog needs to maximize his digestive potential with the use of enzyme therapy, taken both internally and by injection at the site of the ailing disc. Raw grated vegetables and sprouts should be added to the food as sources of additional live enzymes, vitamins, and minerals in a readily available form. The herb comfrey is a most valuable addition to the diet in all bone disorders. The entire matter of diagnosis, diet, and injection should be discussed thoroughly with your vet.

Exercise up and down the stairs should be curtailed temporarily, as it will only serve to put more pressure on the already weakened spinal joint. So the dog should remain on level ground, placing newspapers in the house if necessary, as it can be a toss-up, in severe cases, between temporary paper training and paralysis. As the dog begins to rise and walk on his own, then slow walks on level ground can be encouraged. When the dog is feeling much stronger, you can slowly reintroduce more vigorous exercise, including the resumption of climbing stairs.

Slipped discs don't suddenly appear mysteriously, and they won't subside mysteriously either. If you are taking proper precautions with diet and exercise, the chances of your older dog suffering slipped

Administering pills should be quick and easy. Open the dog's mouth wide, pop the pill deep into his mouth. . .

. . . then, holding the muzzle upward, rub the throat gently. Make certain the pill goes down.

If your dog has a back or leg problem, support him or her as suggested and go for a rehabilitative walk.

discs are happily minimized. Should you also take vital precautions and not allow your dog out without a leash, then you are eliminating the chances of his getting a slipped disc through his being struck by a car. Remember that a slipped disc can lead to paralysis and impairment of vital motor and excretory functions, and this can most certainly lead to death.

There are other mishaps that can affect the spine and the forward or rear legs. Severe calcification of joints can lead to great pain when walking. Hip dysplasia, occurring most frequently in the larger breeds, also impairs the dog's ability to get around. You will have to provide rehabilitation therapy for animals who have imperfect use of their back or front legs. Your job will be to provide much love and patience, and motivation for the dog to persevere and try to get better. As long as the dog has some use of his limbs and some sensation, we can proceed to assist him in walking, with the aid of a strap looped and placed around his body close to the front or rear legs, whichever are most impaired. The strap, which you will hold taut, will serve to take some of the body weight off his legs and allow him to negotiate one step after another to regain some of his lost mobility.

Despite his handicap, this dog enjoys posing for a handsome portrait.

Diet for Bone and Joint Impairments

Animals with bone and joint impairments need massive doses of vitamin C and the bioflavonoids, together with a healthful diet of raw grated vegetables, comfrey herb, sprouts, cottage cheese, ricotta, yogurt, raw milk, buttermilk, kefir, farmer cheese, garlic, kelp, enzymes, lamb, veal, chicken, fish, dry additive-free crunchy dog food, and soft-boiled eggs. Dogs who have walking disabilities, should be watched for overweight. Feed an older dog, or one with disabilities, two or three smaller, highly nutritious meals a day. In this way you will not strain the digestive and elimination systems. Any surplus weight *must* come off, *for obesity is truly a short cut to the grave for man and beast alike.*

Loss of an Eye

Dogs often lose the sight of one or both eyes, through progressive cataracts or the graying in the lens that comes with age. Sometimes a serious impairment such as glaucoma can necessitate the re-

23

moval of one or both eyes. Many people might have a first reaction of revulsion, thinking the removal of an eye to be unesthetic. Beauty is truly in the eyes of the beholder.

Our older dog, Morris, is a beautiful exemplification of an older dog. He has a technical, or medical, handicap in that he is missing an eye. But, psychologically, Morris has great wealth. He has the good fortune to belong to a sensitive, loving, compassionate couple who look upon his infirmity as a minor readjustment to be compensated for collectively. Morris is not made to feel guilty for having lost an eye. He is not made to feel any less adorable or lovable because of this slight deviation in appearance. He is not rebuked if it takes him a little longer to orient himself in strange surroundings. Of course Morris, as other dogs like him, has lost a measure of peripheral vision. This is not a catastrophe to dogs as much as it can be with humans. Morris can compensate adequately with the remaining eye, so long as the family ensures a familiarity for him with his surroundings. If your dog undergoes an operation for the removal of an eye, it would be less than propitious for you to pick that time to redecorate the house or to relocate the family. Morris and his brethren in fate do not have an Adonis mentality or a Narcissus complex. They feel just as handsome with or without the eye.

And well they should. For it is not the trappings of outward appearance that matter in life, but the purity of one's inner self. In the case of Morris, this purity was reflected through his owners' love. Their commitment to his comfort and happiness is what gave his life quality and good fortune. Morris was not thrust into crowds of boisterous people who would startle and anger him with their abrupt movements. He was lavished with love, good food, and familiar surroundings. He basked in the contentment and security of his own special world. If this sounds like a eulogy, it is. Morris' life has run full cycle; he lived and died, sheltered in the bosom of those who loved him most. His memory is forever etched in the thoughts of that unique couple. Now, befitting a special dog and his special people, Morris has attained immortality through this book.

The handicapped dog is always a special dog. He needs special considerations. If his diet was adequate, it must be even better now. If his diet was poor, it is paramount to start feeding him a maximum stress diet now. The handicapped dog is under extra stress both psychologically and physically. Infirmity is nothing to be ashamed of, but neither is it something to be ignored, or reviewed with great remorse. Change what can be changed and become adjusted to what cannot. Flux is the nature of life. So is uncertainty. If your dog becomes handicapped, treat him with love, compassion, and intelligence. If you manage that, your dog will be among the most fortunate of his kind.

When you must remove an object from your dog's mouth, pour some Granick's "Bitter Apple" on the item . . .

. . . it can then be easily removed from the mouth.

Chapter III

GENERAL HEALTH CARE

Teeth

Dogs are very often afflicted with tooth troubles as they advance in years. You should understand what is happening when, seemingly for no reason, your pet's mouth has teeth that are swimming in their sockets. We know that dogs don't very often get cavities, but they most certainly do get gingivitis (inflammation of the gums) and periodontal disease (the breakdown of gingival [gum] tissues surrounding the tooth, as well as the gradual destruction of the underlying tooth structure itself). Older dogs are very prone to tooth loss from periodontal disease, an affliction that frequently affects older people as well, and for essentially the same reasons. Deterioration of gum and bone tissue manifests itself as swollen bleeding gums, offensive mouth odors, and loose teeth. The dog will find it painful to chew, and so you may see an accompanying loss of appetite.

Periodontal disease is an infection characterized by excessive plaque formation. Plaque is a film of mucus that provides a shelter for bacteria. Dogs don't brush their teeth, so they are unable to remove the retained food particles that give nourishment for bacteria. Dental plaque on and around the tooth surfaces is formed by certain bacteria that produce dextran, a sticky, gummy substance that gives to plaque its adhesive strength. Other varieties of bacteria are subsequently attracted to this sticky substance, and they proceed to multiply by the billions. Plaque eventually mineralizes and becomes hardened, at which time it is known as calculus or tartar. Layers of new plaque are then formed on the tartar, which cause the surrounding gums to pull back from their attachments to the enamel surfaces of the teeth. This invasion continues until the bacteria excrete acidlike toxins that actually destroy the supporting structure. At this point, the teeth loosen from their sockets (a condition known as pyorrhea), and they will then either fall out or they will have to be extracted.

27

Dream enjoys chewing on natural hard bones and rawhide twists. Rubber toys with squeaks should be avoided. Sterilized natural bones, "Nylabone," and "Nylaball" are some of the best chew toys for dogs of all ages. They are safe and economical because they last.

To prevent the development of an excessive plaque colony, a wholesome diet of raw vegetables, raw meat, crunchy kibble, and natural bones will help to keep the teeth and gums in good condition. Vitamin C complex is very important in building up collagen, the cement of cells, in cases of peridontal disease. Vitamins A and D are important: A keeps infections down and D helps calcium to work better.

If your dog does build up excess tartar, have it removed by your vet. This will minimize the occurrence of gum inflammation. If teeth are slightly loose, try megavitamin and mineral therapy before opting to pull them. But if they are so loose that they cause great discomfort, then you probably have no choice but to extract them.

Dogs do not develop caries (cavities) as readily as do humans, because the surface of their tooth enamel is more resistant to the primary bacteria that cause caries. Incidentally, it is neither necessary nor advisable to eliminate all bacteria from the oral surfaces. It has been estimated that approximately sixty percent of the bacteria in the oral cavity of both humans and animals is comprised of harmless or friendly bacterial flora. Some of this flora is needed for proper digestion. A dog's saliva varies in thickness, according to what type of food he must negotiate. The elimination of all bacteria, both friendly and unfriendly, could also create a mouth fungus.

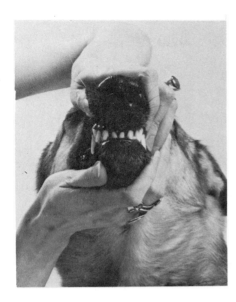 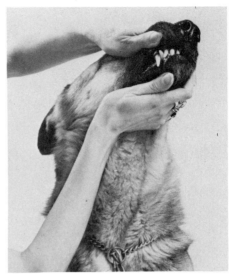

Check your dog's teeth regularly for tartar buildup. Raw fruits and vegetables will help minimize plaque formation. Do not use bone meal or dolomite supplements. In their crude form, they can cause more problems than they correct. Calcium gluconate and oratate are more assimilable, as is raw carrot and turnip juice.

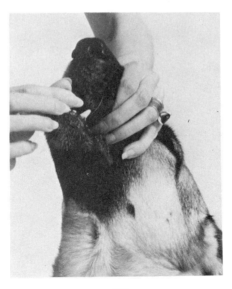

Bad breath, as associated with bad teeth, is the result of the action of disease-producing bacteria on decaying or putrefying food in the mouth. They release toxins and cause corrosive damage to mouth surfaces. If you either clean away the food, thereby starving the harmful bacteria, or you provide a healthful, self-cleaning diet, the incidence of periodontal disease in your dog will be reduced.

Diet has a great deal to do with your pet's oral health. Refined, soft, mushy foods will allow tooth surfaces to become coated with putrefying food. This develops a vigorous and thriving plaque colony. Keep your dog's diet as close as possible to what nature had intended and he will have much less chance of trouble with his teeth.

Eyes

As a dog becomes older, his eyes reveal more ills. Many infections and diseases first show as changes in the eyes. This should indicate to you that eye problems often are not necessarily local irritations but a manifestation of some problem elsewhere in the body. Jaundice, a liver disease where bile is backing up and closing off the bile duct, due to some obstruction such as a stone or worm, is revealed by a yellowness in the eyes. Excessive brightness in the whites of the eyes can reveal anemia. Weeping eyes can signal allergies. Twitching eyes can be precursors of stroke, or indicate concussions. Chronic nephritis (kidney inflammation) shows up in the retina as hemorrhage. Cataracts can signal diabetes. But in no case should these be areas for lay diagnosis. Your vet should be the one to diagnose.

Eyelids are subject to inflammations, sometimes through mange which is a skin fungus. Warts can grow on or under the eyelid, causing the dog considerable discomfort. In older dogs, eyelids sometimes roll inward, irritating the eyeball. Some dogs have a double row of lashes, the one set curling inward against the eyeball. Often situations like this are corrected with surgery. Conjunctivivitis is an inflammation of the conjunctiva of the eye (the mucus membrane that covers the front of the eyeball). This can be caused by cuts, scratches, foreign bodies, insect bites, or bee stings.

Many older dogs begin to develop an opacity in the lens of the eye called a cataract. You will begin to notice a cloudiness covering the surface of the eye, where it used to be quite clear. Cataracts have their origins in nutritional deficiencies, being an accumulation of toxic debris that settles on the surface of the lens. This often occurs with diabetes and, being linked with diabetes, indicates that the animal is probably a sugarholic being fed on semimoist foods and other sugar-saturated fare. Cataracts are unfortunately all too common in the older dog.

With age, a dog will begin to develop a grayish tinge in the pupils of the eye. This graying usually begins after the fifth or sixth year. The lens itself is changing and becoming more opaque, but this is not a cataract. If you see any changes in the appearance of your dog's eyes, call your vet for a proper diagnosis.

Eyes may be bathed in several types of herbal solutions if discharging or weeping becomes a problem. Chamomile or fennel tea or the juice of raw cucumbers are three soothing options that may be used to keep the eyes clear and healthy. Boric acid solution is also used, as are several commercial preparations, but a wipe with plain water on a cotton pad, in maintenance situations, is all that is needed.

Keeping the eye ducts clear of excess buildup is very important. It will keep your dog comfortable and healthy.

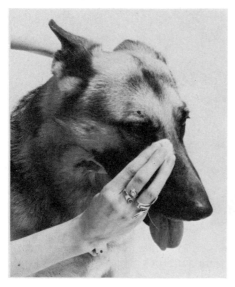 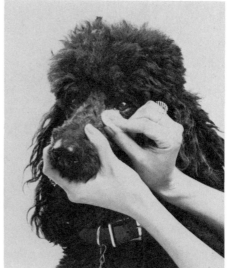

Ears

The ears are composed of three parts: the external, which is the flap and canal leading to the eardrum; the middle ear, the cavity behind the drum, which contains vibrating bones that move in reponse to varying pressure; and the inner ear, which contains nerves leading to the brain and semicircular canals that control balance. Very few problems of the ear can be considered really grave, but there are many annoying problems that may have to be dealt with in the older dog.

Ear cankers can be common in dogs with long floppy ears that prohibit healthy circulation of air. Some cankers must be corrected by surgery, because heredity has narrowed the ear passage to the shutting out of all air. In such case, an air duct has to be created through surgery. Long floppy ears can be cleaned with an herbal mixture of steeped rosemary leaves at three parts to one part of witch hazel. For an alternative, diluted witch hazel can be used plain. Ear cankers have responded to treatment with raw, freshly squeezed lemon juice in the ratio of one half teaspoon of juice to one half tablespoon of warm water. When ear cankers are the result of parasites, then an insecticide should be used. Ears are extremely sensitive and should not be subjected to excess poking and prodding. If you are in doubt about your ability to handle a situation, let your vet handle it. He or

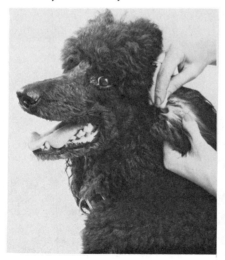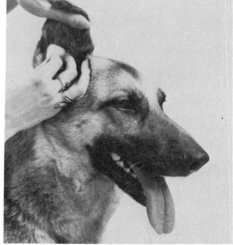

Keep the ears free from waxy buildup.Use cotton balls soaked in baby oil or peroxide. Resist the urge to use Q-tips because they might penetrate the ear canal too deeply.

she has far more experience than you in such matters and will not create undue fear or resistance in your dog.

Ear hematomas (a tumor or swelling filled with blood) are caused by dogs shaking their heads vigorously, whereby the tips hit some solid object, rupturing the delicate veins inside. Blood collects in a pocket under the skin. Very often there is no external bleeding. In time, blood is often resorbed, but sometimes the hematoma must be surgically treated to allow proper healing to take place. If the hematoma is very big, the dog may end up with a cauliflower ear, with or without surgery.

Warts can develop on or in the ear. If they lodge deep inside the ear canal, they can set up a general infection. So they should be removed before they create any serious problems.

Dogs, especially poodles, are prone to growing excess hair in the ear. Such a mat of hair can impair circulation of air and increase the potential for infection. Dogs with this problem should have excess hair plucked out regularly by your groomer.

Dogs in general suffer a certain degree of hearing loss as they get older. They accept it, for the most part, as normal, even though the owner is rarely aware of such loss. The dog interprets the situation as simply that sounds are getting softer, not that he is getting hard of hearing. Deafness can also be caused by specific diseases, or by blockages and growths. If these last are attended to, the dog can enjoy amazing revitalization of his hearing.

Nails

The older dog's nails tend to grow longer not because they are growing faster, but because the dog is getting less exercise and thereby is not wearing them down as much. You can make a conscious effort to walk your dog on some hard surface daily so his nails won't grow too fast. You can also take him to the vet or to the groomer more often, so he will not suffer the discomfort of long nails. Beware of trying to clip your dog's nails yourself. There is a vein called the quick that runs through the nails. (It is easier to see on blond nails than on dark ones.) Should the quick be cut accidentally, you will have a fair amount of bleeding to stop, you will have caused considerable discomfort to your dog, and you will probably have turned off your dog permanently to the benefits of a manicure. If the dog's nails click when he walks, or even if they touch the floor, then they are too long, and in need of clipping. Long, jagged nails can cause an infection on other parts of the body when the dog scratches

Check the anal glands regularly. If you cannot do it yourself, have your veterinarian express them.

just for the fun of it, and he may develop minor abrasions as a result of his nails being too long and too rough. Under no circumstances should you allow the nails to turn under, causing him more pain when walking than he would normally experience with his gradually stiffening joints.

Anal Glands

Also called the "scent glands" or "anal sacs," the anal glands are positioned to either side of and slightly below the anus. They contain a fluid secretion that normally is discharged into, then out through the anus. In older dogs the secretion tends to collect in the sac, becoming thick, gummy, and offensive in odor. The impacted fluid causes the dog discomfort and makes him drag his rear end on the ground or lick his genitals to excess. If your dog has the problem of fluid retention in the anal sacs, then by all means attend to it, both for his comfort and for your own peace of mind. The material can be expressed by your vet, or he can perhaps show you how to do it. However, the contents of the sac can always be more completely expressed (removed) by the vet, and sometimes there may be duct obstruction or rupture in the sac that could cause abscesses.

Many people misdiagnose anal gland congestion as worms when a dog reacts by dragging his rear end along the ground. Occasionally the problem is worms but, with the older dog, it more likely is anal gland impaction. When neglected, anal sacs can become infected, leading to more trouble. Chronic licking of these infected parts can lead to infections in the mouth and on other parts of the body. Herbal therapy includes the application of dandelion brew (leaves and flowers) or fenugreek seeds, two tablespoons to one cup warm water, then give the liquid as a drink and use the seeds mixed in with food. Linseed tea is also used internally and externally, and witch hazel can be applied topically. You can combine a few different therapies and arrive at what works best for you.

Skin

The skin is the largest eliminative organ in the body, being much larger in surface area than the lungs, liver, kidneys, and large intestine combined. The skin also includes the mucus membranes that line body cavities such as the nose, mouth, eyes, and digestive tract. The skin has many functions other than the obvious one of holding the dog together. It is a barometer of general health.

Diet is related to a great many skin problems. Even parasites, which we tend to think of as an external problem, are related to diet. Parasites prefer to pray on diseased flesh. Their function is to eventually eliminate an unhealthy organism by doing what they do best: devouring it. The healthier your dog is, the less his skin will provide the succulent odor, the taste, and the ideal breeding ground for parasites to thrive. This also applies to the internal parasites that thrive in mucus-filled, fecal-infested colons.

Charcoal tablets or bones will help to purify the intestinal tract. They are useful, too, in controlling worms. The charcoal helps absorb the impurities from internal organs, but they should be used only intermittently as they can leach out nourishment as well as impurities.

It is important to feed the older dog a good, high-biological-value source of proteins; fats; whole-grain carbohydrates; fresh raw, grated vegetables; together with an ample supply of the proper vitamins, minerals, enzymes, and friendly bacterial flora so necessary to maintain a properly stable internal condition in the body. See to it that your dog has the proper natural, unrefined, saturated and unsaturated fatty acids in his diet to keep his skin healthy But even a balanced diet cannot provide optimum results if the dog's disgestive system is malfunctioning so that he is unable to utilize the nutrients. Digestive problems can show up in a large variety of skin disorders.

Thyroid, kidney, or liver malfunctions can also cause skin problems. Bile or pancreatic dysfunctions can lead to skin problems, as will the glands that produce various hormones if they begin to malfunction in the older dog. Once the cause is isolated, it usually is a relatively simple matter to correct a skin problem, but finding the actual cause out of a myriad of possibilities is very often a time-consuming and frustrating search.

Give your dog a bath when he gets dirty. This of course will vary with the dog and with the conditions under which he lives. Brush him daily, or several times weekly, to stimulate the scalp, reduce flaking, and discourage matting. Longer-coated dogs will need to be brushed more frequently than short-coated dogs. With these attentions, plus a good, wholesome, balanced, nutritious diet, you will be minimizing the possibilities of any skin disease cropping up to make your older dog miserable.

Allergies

Animals can be allergic both to foods and nonfoods. Highly allergenic foods (that create allergies) are beef, wheat, corn, and tap water (which can contain a fungus); other foods allergenic in lesser proportion are horsemeat, eggs, milk, fish, chicken, lamb, veal, and mutton. Some animals have been found to be allergic to all animal protein, and an animal can be allergic to any food. This doesn't necessarily signify that the food is bad. It is only bad for him.

If you suspect your dog has a food allergy, change his diet completely, to something like lamb, cottage cheese, soybeans, barley, brown rice, carrots, and garlic. Try this for two weeks, also using only bottled spring water in case your dog is allergic to impurities in the water, of which there are many. If your dog's allergy subsides or disappears, you can be reasonably sure you have an FIH (food-induced-hypersensitivity) problem. Continue the new diet until all symptoms disappear, if possible. Then slowly reintroduce one of the old food items each week, until your dog again develops a reaction. Keep a record of everything you feed him and when, so that, at the point where you do get a reaction, you will be able to know what food you last added that caused the reaction, and again remove that food from the diet for another week or two. To be absolutely sure a particular food is allergenic to your dog, reintroduce the same food a second time, after the two-week absence. If your dog reacts a second time, then that food item should be taken permanently from his diet. Follow this same procedure with every food that was part of his old diet, including the water. If he develops a reaction twice, you know there is no mistake about the particular food. Dogs that are allergic to

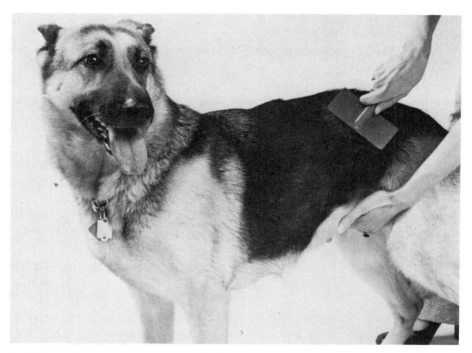

Daily brushing is important for all breeds. Brush against the grain of the fur . . . and then with it. Natural bristle brushes are very good for stimulating the skin surface, and "slicker" brushes (as shown) do a good job of removing loose hairs.

food are usually allergic to more than one food.

Dogs also become allergic to external substances such as pollen, house dust, wool, and synthetic fibers. Some vets feel that if the allergy, (welts, blemishes, hair loss) is symmetrical, it is probably dietary, whereas if it is not symmetrical, it is more often caused by an external environmental factor. This is an interesting theory, but no one has bothered to explain the rationale behind it. Whatever the allergy, it is within all of our capabilities to test for food as the possible causative factor.

With environmental allergies, perhaps the best way to determine the cause is by skin testing, sometimes called scratch testing. (You may have to go to a veterinary school for elaborate testing of this kind, such as the one at Cornell, since they generally have very complete facilities.) Once the cause is isolated, the dog can usually be desensitized by injections. Sometimes the dog is allergic to a wool blanket in the car or on the couch where he sleeps, or to goose down, kapok, or other bedding material. He may be allergic to a synthetic carpet, or to the wax or a cleaner you use on the kitchen tiles. Try switching the place where he sleeps long enough to find out if any of these changes help. If you are fortunate, you will find the culprit. Otherwise you'll have to go the expensive, time-consuming, skin-test routine.

One of the worst things that can happen to a dog, is for him to become allergic to a part of his own anatomy. The prognosis for this type of allergy is not very good, Animals, like humans, also can be allergic to bee stings, flies, fleas, ticks, and mites. Any of these can cause an allergic reaction.

By watching your dog's food intake and being alert to his external environment, you can go a long way toward preventing allergies.

Clothing

People differ diametrically about clothing for the older dog, and opinions are usually vehement on both sides. Some take the position that a dog has is own natural coat, that clothing is sissified and emascualtes a dog—the raincoats, plaid all-weather coats, and the like. These people especially reject clothing for big dogs such as the Shepherd, Doberman, or St. Bernard. Although a Toy Poodle or Shih Tzu walking down the street in custom-made clothes is apt to elicit a favorable comment from passers by, the big dog who is similarly attired will more likely receive scorn or ridicule. The people who are particularly in favor of coats and boots are usually the ones who make them, so we cannot expect great objectivity from them. However, many owners enjoy this indulgence and there is no harm in it. Small dogs seem to enjoy all the pampering that goes with dressing to go out. But, if outer clothing were a true essential for ALL dogs, why are there so few in larger sizes? The owner of a big masculine-looking dog simply is not prepared psychologically to accept the idea. He sees clothing as a waste of time, money, and effort, as well as an embarrassment to himself.

In fairness to both sides, clothing does provide a certain amount of insulation against cold weather. It serves to cushion the extremes of temperature between a very warm house and the severe cold outside. The anticlothing faction say that dogs stay out in the cold all the time, without ever needing clothing. But they have answered the question why without realizing it. Dogs who stay out all the time are not subjected to the temperature fluctuations that can bring on illness in a vulnerable dog. It is not so much the temperature but the severe change in temperature that can be dangerous. Dogs that are outside all the time develop a very thick coat naturally, to insulate them from the extreme cold. Dogs that are in a warm, dry home or apartment most of the time will shed more and maintain a thinner coat, accommodating to the warmer temperature. It is the extremes from heat to cold that can cause a susceptible dog to catch a chill or fall ill, and the older dog already had more trouble regulating his body heat. So, for these reasons there can be some rationale to the winter coat and the raincoat for any dog whose owner desires this protection. With clothing you can moderate the extreme temperature shock your dog may experience in very severe weather.

Boots are also a debatable issue among dog owners and dog fan-

After walking your dog outside in any questionable substance such as rock salt or antifreeze, wash off his or her paws. Then lubricate them with vaseline.

39

ciers. Proponents of boots for dogs will argue that boots keep the house cleaner but, more importantly, they protect the dog from the harmful, irritating effects of rock salt and antifreeze solutions upon his feet. This is true. A dog's paws are porous, and through the pores of their feet they can absorb many irritating substances, even to affecting internal organs. They can also have a hard time walking on ice. Some lose their footing, fall, and injure themselves. A dog's paws will often stick to cold, hard ice and/or rock salt, causing severe pain and irritation.

All this can be avoided with boots. That doesn't mean boots every day of the winter, but using boots on very severe, cold, icy days can save your dog a lot of discomfort and perhaps illness. Dogs who find it painful to walk on ice and rock salt will be less inclined to relieve themselves when walked. This can cause constipation, bladder problems, and accidents in the house, all of which can be avoided. Dogs who walk unprotected on ice and rock salt will frequently develop a limp and painful lacerations on the paws which their owners rarely associate with the weather conditions.

Taking all of the above into consideration, you may now see dog clothing in a different light. Do whatever seems right for you and for the safety and protection of your older dog. That is always the most important consideration.

Grooming

Grooming should always be done on a regular basis. If you have a low-maintenance dog such as a Shepherd or Doberman, then most of the grooming can be handled by you. But if you have a high-maintenance dog such as a Poodle or Old English Sheepdog, then much of the grooming will have to be done by a professional. It is unfair both to your dog and to the groomer to neglect the animal until he is all matted up, and then expect the groomer to perform a miracle without the dog suffering. Even if the groomer charges you more for this neglect, and he has a perfect right to do so, what he and the dog have to go through is not worth it. Imagine combing *your* hair with an egg beater, then trying to pull out the tangles; after a very short time you will be quite willing to get a Telly Savalas bob. So appreciate the suffering your dog will have to endure if he is not brushed and combed regularly, and has to withstand a painful, tedious session at the groomer.

There is no way to compensate for neglect except to strip the dog down almost to his bare skin. You may not mind if he resembles

All animals are happier and healthier when well-groomed. Ms. "Pooh Fat" knows she is beautiful! Pooh is also a complete vegetarian, eating all salads and dairy products with no commercial foods.

a giant water rat with floppy ears, but you should. The time to think about low or high maintenance with a dog is before you have him. Once he is part of your household, it is your responsibility to do what is best for him, regardless of the slight inconvenience to you.

Early detection of any unusual lumps or skin problems is more likely to occur with dogs that go regularly to a professional groomer. Eye and tooth troubles are also very often detected by an observant groomer. This is not the primary reason to go to the groomer, and it doesn't replace going to the vet, but it is another side benefit of regular maintenance.

Dogs should be bathed as often as necessary. This doesn't mean x-many times a year, but only as often as necessary. Try to find a natural herbal shampoo with pennyroyal oil used as a natural flea repellent. We discourage the use of flea collars because of the poisons they contain and the damage they can do to the dog. You can sprinkle pennyroyal and/or eucalyptus leaves on the dog's bedding, or use the oils of these herbs rubbed into the dog's coat for protection. A final bath rinse of diluted lemon juice in water or cider vinegar in water will serve to return the skin to its proper pH. A dog's skin should not be as acid as a human's, but many shampoos are too alkaline and leave the animal with a dry, flaky, itching skin. Lemon juice or cider vinegar will lower the pH and minimize drying, itching, and flaking.

Basic grooming maintenance is a very small price to pay for all the joy and affection your dog bestows upon you throughout his lifetime. This responsibility is basic to owning a dog and should never be shirked—for the sake of your dog.

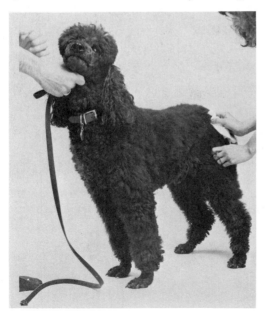

To restrain a dog's muzzle for removal of ticks or examination for other parasites or disorders, wrap the leash several turns around the muzzle and hold firmly.

Chapter IV

DISEASES AND COMPLAINTS OF THE AGING DOG

Abrasions

Abrasions are often caused by scratching and biting skin surfaces that itch. Herbal treatments include an infusion (brew) of blackberry leaves, rosemary leaves, or elder flowers and leaves to which a little witch hazel has been added. Apply topically to abrasions. It is suggested that no greasy preparations be used, for they will retain moisture on the skin surfaces and retard healing.

Abscesses

Abscesses are the body's attempt to throw off through the skin toxins from impure blood. Blood that is excessively toxic is choked and is unable to carry away the waste matter of cell metabolism through its normal channels. Thus white blood cells surround disease-producing bacteria and toxic waste and carry them out of the body through the skin in the form of pus. If your dog is bothered by many abscesses at one time, or by frequent growths, he should be fasted for several days on distilled water and *raw* honey (to keep up his energy): two to four teaspoonsful a day, depending upon the size of the dog. As the dog begins to eliminate more toxins, give several garlic cloves daily in with his food. Garlic will help him to detoxify even more. Hot fomentations (packs) of blackberry leaves, groundsel, or elderberry, may be put on the abscesses. Or you can use chopped-up garlic or onion or both, heated in several ounces of castor oil. Heat it in a pan of water till comfortably hot, and then apply as hot packs. Nutrients that may be helpful in treating abscesses are vitamins A, C, and E, and B complex, red clover, cayenne pepper,

43

chapparal, goldenseal, and carrots or potatoes (grated and applied as poultices).

Anemia

Anemia is basically a lack of hemoglobin and oxygen in the blood. It is often caused by faulty diet, lack of exposure to sunlight, and a constipation of the entire system, including the lower bowel. The dog may become weak and faint, losing energy and stamina. His eyes may show excessive brightness in the white portion. Internal parasites may weaken a dog, causing severe anemia. Anemia can be caused by too little blood or too few red cells. If you check your dog's gums, they will be whiter than normal, upon pressure, and slow to return to a pink color.

Or your dog may lack sufficient iron in his diet; toxins produced by many diseases can cause an anemic condition. To boost the iron in his diet, you can give your dog desiccated liver, brewers' yeast, and blackstrap molasses in with his food. You can also give berries or fruits of the black variety including bramble (blackberry), bilberry, elderberry, or grapes. Honey is also good, as are eggs, kelp, and parsley. Other nutrients that may be helpful in cases of anemia are vitamins C, E, and the B complex, protein, and copper and iron. Chemical iron aggravates anemia and cause constipation.

Arthritis

Arthritis has become a common ailment in dogs, especially the older dog; many factors contribute to this condition, including an all-cooked-food diet, lack of exercise, poor absorption of minerals, and lack of hydrochloric acid in the stomach. It occurs as an inflamation in bones and joints. The onset is gradual and the owner notices the dog having increased difficulty in walking, getting up, lying down, running, and moving in general.

Putting an arthritic dog on distilled water exclusively will help to leach out some of the mineral deposits that have settled in the joints. Your dog also needs a live-food diet. You may use a good-quality dry kibble as a base, but along with it give your dog plenty of sprouts, grated raw vegetables, garlic, and raw fruits, all of which are alkalizing to the body. Meats and grains are acid-forming for the most part, and an arthritic dog already has too much acid in his diet. Any meat should be raw to slightly braised. Give chopped comfrey and parsley leaves in with the food. Keep the dog in a warm, dry place, and try to give him some moderate exercise in sunlight. You can feed rosemary leaves daily as an infusion (steep them in water), or boiled nettles. The inflamed areas can be massaged with four tablespoonsful of olive oil, (raw, unrefined), one tablespoonful of linseed oil, and one-half teaspoon of eucalyptus oil. Nutrients that may be beneficial in treating arthritis are vitamins A, B complex, C, D, E, and F; calcium, iodine, lecithin, magnesium, phosphorus, potassium, sulfur, and protein.

Bad Breath

Bad breath is often caused by a constipated digestive system, locking in putrefying toxic wastes. This comes from having too much dead, refined food and not enough raw, live food or fiber (roughage) in the diet. A sluggish system will give back the stench of indigestion, all the way back up to the mouth again. A dog can be constipated even if he has a daily movement. In fact, pitifully few dogs aren't constipated throughout their lifetime, although this is rarely evident to their owners. Infusions of rosemary leaves and flowers, lemon juice and water, apple juice, *raw* honey, and a short fast (several days) will all serve to sweeten up the intestines. Regular fasting, one day a week, on distilled water and *raw* honey, will help to rest the digestive organs on a regular basis, giving them a chance to catch up on their contents. Use lots of raw fruits and vegetables in the diet, give yogurt and kefir to reinstate the friendly bacterial flora, and feed only raw or slightly braised meat.

Baldness

A chronic slow loss of hair, due to ill health, is sometimes found in older dogs. Feed a diet of raw foods: meats, vegetables, and fruits. Give brewers' yeast, kelp, and desiccated liver. Add raw corn, olive, peanut, or safflower oil to the food for unsaturated fatty acids. Chopped dandelion leaves (high in copper) may be added to the food. Balding areas can be bathed daily with an infusion of rosemary leaves, marigold flowers, or daffodil leaves. Castor and eucalyptus oil can also be massaged into the balding areas.

Breast Tumors

Breat tumors often occur in unspayed female dogs, though this is not, in our opinion, a blanket reason to spay them. Tumors are very often caused by hormonal imbalances and changes, together with a general state of toxemia and ill health. The breast tumor can be linked with an estrogen factor. Tumors on any part of the body are

45

the body's attempt to localize and isolate some disease condition. "Tumor" means swelling, and tumors are benign or malignant by classification. In reality, a tumor is often benign in certain of its areas and malignant in others. Biopsies can aggravate the malignant portion of tumors, sometimes causing their rapid spreading. Tumor specialists realize that very often the larger the tumor, the smaller the malignant portion in porportion to the nonmalignant or benign portion.

By cutting out the tumor or tumors, one is only removing the local indications of the disease. Nothing is being done about the cause. In many cases the cause has not even been sought for or recognized. Therapies that will decrease or dry up a tumor can also serve to prevent them. It is not as important to remove a tumor that is not pressing on a vital organ as it is to stop its spread. Nonorthodox treatments such as Laetrile have been used to arrest the spread, even though they did not significantly reduce the size of the tumor. It is the spread of a malignancy that kills, more often than the size of the tumor itself. Removing the toxic or poisonous quality is all-important in treating a tumor, malignant or otherwise. A diet rich in live, raw foods, will serve to supply vital enzymes to the body. Enzyme therapy may be indicated along with raw foods. More information can be obtained on enzymes and other nontoxic therapies from THE INTERNATIONAL ASSOCIATION OF CANCER VICTIMS AND FRIENDS, 7740 W. Manchester Ave. #110 Playa del Rey, California, 90291, and also from THE COMMITTEE FOR FREEDOM OF CHOICE IN CANCER THERAPY, 146 Main Street, Suite 408, Los Altos, California, 94072.

A theory on cancer that seems most valid among nutritional circles is that cancer is partly caused by faulty protein metabolization. By changing to a raw, live-food diet, you will give the blood a chance to clarify itself. A clean blood stream means a healthy body. A diseased, choked-up blood stream can breed nothing but disease. Herbal therapies include blue violet leaves, red clover, chapparal, goldenseal, garlic, and turnip used both internally and as a poultice; goose grass as a poultice; burdock, dandelion root, slippery elm, comfrey, blue flag, and poke root as a poultice and a tea. Three excellent herbal reference books are *Back to Eden* by Jethro Kloss, *The Complete Herbal Book for the Dog* by Juliette de Bairacli Levy, and *Healing Animals with Herbs* by John Heinerman. Dr. John Craige, a veterinarian in Monterey, California, has done some very important research with Laetrile and other nontoxic methods in the treatment of cancer and other metabolic diseases in dogs and cats. If you write to him, he will probably arrange to have his published articles sent to you.

Cancer

Cancer is a universal disease whose very mention strikes fear and horror in the hearts of men. Cancer strikes one out of four humans. While figures are not that gruesome yet for pets, more dogs are dying of cancer now than they did ten years ago. Cancer sometimes has a very grim outcome for pets, especially in the areas of the liver and spleen. Very few people have the inclination or the money necessary to go through the time-consuming therapy or the series of operations for their pet that may be deemed advisable in the case of a cancer. The disease is degenerative in nature: it does not strike down your dog from the blue. Cancer is a long time gestating in subclinical stages before it manifests as clinical. Many factors can be involved. The mind is an important component in any indicated cancer. Negative, unhappy, resentful dogs are more likely to become cancerous than happy, well-adjusted, secure animals. Stress is an important element in the growth of cancer. Above all, cancer can be caused by and aggravated by bad nutrition.

Most animals today eat a diet of all-dead, highly refined, highly chemicalized foods. This diet fails to nourish the cells of the body properly and sets up the climate for cancer. Cancer doesn't happen in a healthy body. The body has to become weakened and in a diseased state before cancer becomes clinical. When researchers implant cancerous tissues into healthy animals, for experimental purposes, the cancers will not take. It is only when experimenters proceed to disease the surrounding tissues that a cancer will then "take" successfully and begin to spread.

Cancer is also a sign of a clogged colon. This may seem amusingly abstract to some people, but among nonspecialist physicians, general practitioners, who deal through nature with the state of cancer, they find an ever-present component to be a state of degeneration in the large intestine. Poor diets cause our pets' digestive apparatus to go completely out of kilter. Soggy dead-food diets make a soggy death trap of the colon. It loses much of its peristaltic motility. The colon becomes encrusted with hardened fecal matter; gas fermentation forms from incomplete digestion of starches, from wrong food combinations, clogged bile ducts, etc. Gas pressure builds up and blows out craters in the large intestines called diverticuli. Hardened, encrusted fecal matter, many years old, lays solidly plastered to the walls of the intestines.

Heavy meat and starch diets encourage the formation of mucus in the system. Thick mucus attaches like icing to the walls of the intestine, making poor absorption of nutrients the next problem. At this point you could feed your animal the best of diets and he could still starve to death, because nutrients are not being absorbed through the walls of the intestine. By indiscriminate combining of foods, the pancreas, part of whose function is to produce digestive enzymes, becomes overtaxed. It no longer has enough enzymes to digest all the incoming food and, since the food is almost always dead, the food has no enzymes of its own to help in the digestive process. The stomach has become more alkaline, having lost the proper secretion of hydrochloric acid; meat cannot digest well in an alkaline environment. So, what happens? The meat begins to spoil or putrefy inside the body. It stores its toxins in the most vulnerable areas of the body.

Friendly bacterial flora also need an acid environment to thrive. In the septic state of the stomach and large intestines, both of which should be acid, the friendly flora lose out to disease-producing bacteria. A disease state takes over because the friendly flora can no longer keep the others in check or help in the digestion of food. Since the pancreas is not functioning properly, trouble does not end there. The pituitary and the pineal glands go awry. Over-response takes place (hyperactivity) until they work themselves into a state of utter exhaustion. Then they cannot supply adequate secretions to the body and they become underactive. At this point we think of glandular substances to stimulate them or to compensate partially for their depleted function. Blood sugar becomes low when the insulin in the pancreas overreacts. Then the adrenal glands overwork to bring the blood sugar back to normal. When the pancreas has exhausted its ability to lower the sugar, because of overreaction and because it had too much of a poor-quality sugar to handle at one time, then it becomes completely unable to function and the blood sugar remains high. That is, unless we give the patient daily shots of insulin and a controlled diet.

All of these, and many more situations, are metabolic disorders that can definitely lead to cancer. But things are not so grim. There is literally no end to the help we can give our pets if only we become aware of the alternatives.

If your animal is stricken with cancer, do not despair. Try to find a vet who practices preventive medicine rather than crisis medicine, who looks at his patients from an allover perspective of nutrition and the whole body. There are lists of these doctors all across the country. Feed your pet entirely on fresh, raw, live foods. Investigate pancreatic-enzyme therapy; Harry Hoxey herbal therapy; enema therapy, both high colonic and coffee enema; juice therapy; oxygen therapy; Max Gerson liver-juice therapy; fasting therapy; orthomolecular vitamin-mineral therapy; glandular therapy; wheatgrass therapy (at the Hippocrates Health Institute in Boston, Massachusetts: Ann Wigmore, proprietor and specialist in cancer and nutrition for animals). There are many roads to health. Familiarize yourself with as many as possible *before* there is an urgent need. You'll be helping your pet and your whole family, and you'll be preventing all those you love from being victimized by cancer. Nutrients that may be beneficial in the treatment of cancer are vitamins A, B complex, C, D, E, and K; iron, phosphorus, potassium; and enzymes.

Cataracts

Cataracts are a common ailment in an older dog (see also Chapter III, under *Eyes*). Toxins in the body have created a localized opacity or whitening in the lens of the eye. Light passing through the lens is reduced and this also reduces the vision proportionately. Cataracts don't always lead to blindness. Sometimes they develop only in one eye or in both at different rates. Operations can be performed on dogs, as they are on people. You can even get contact lenses for dogs, though we don't know how practical this would be.

Vitamin A is very important for eye disorders. Give your animal plenty of raw, grated carrots and parsley in cases of cataracts. Since cataracts are associated with diabetes, you will want to keep refined sugars and starches out of the diet. Vitamin A is plentiful in liver, which may be given raw two or three times a week. Vitamin A is also abundant in cod liver oil, halibut oil, raw milk, and eggs. Herbalists use an infusion of celandine leaves and flowers, rosemary, chickweed, mallow flowers, or dock leaves. These herbs can be used as a bath for the eyes. You can also use rue flowers or sage leaves or raw cucumber juice to bathe the eyes. Nutrients that may be beneficial in treatment of cataracts are vitamins A, B complex, C, D, and E, calcium, and protein.

Constipation

Dogs become constipated primarily from faulty diets. When the bowels do not move regularly, it becomes more difficult for each subsequent movement since fecal matter is creating blockages. Sometimes a large tumor in the prostate of an older dog can exert great pressure on the colon, leading to severe constipation. Even an arthritic condition could cause constipation. If the dog finds it difficult to get around, he may also be disinclined toward answering nature's call. Overweight dogs are more likely to become constipated. Insufficient bile production can lead to constipation. Older dogs should be walked more often, to help guard against constipation.

In very extreme cases, where the constipation has been chronic for a long time, the use of a series of high colonic irrigations (enemas) can be very helpful when nothing else works. Colonics have dissolved severe impactions that would have had to be removed surgically by incision into the colon. Irrigation is a form of water therapy, but unfortunately it is hard enough to find a colonic therapist for humans and even more difficult to locate one for animals. The series of irrigations will serve to loosen up encrusted fecal matter that no normal enema or laxative ever could. Colonics transport water and herbs, often with coconut oil, all the way up the descending colon, across the transverse colon, and down to the ascending colon, stopping at the ileocecal valve which is the flexure between the small and large intestines. It is not only the water, but pressure, volume, control going in and out, herbs, time, and manual massage that all help to make it work like nothing else can. Heat lamps are often used to relax the muscles before a colonic, and the large intestine is massaged while its contents are soaking in water to soften up the fecal matter. After you have unblocked the colon in this way, you will tremendously increase absorption of nutrients. The body does not heal selectively. When you begin to detoxify the body, all ailments begin to minimize and improve. For intermediate relief, and in the case of cancer, a perked-coffee enema will be very useful. The caffeine serves to stimulate the liver as well as the peristaltic action of the intestines. But enemas are not meant to be taken forever. Once the initial problem is corrected, maintaining a proper diet will prevent constipation from recurring. Corrective diet is the only sure cure.

Herbal relief can be obtained with senna pods or senna powder, psyllium seed, flaxseed, any of which can be added to food, milk, or juice. Fruits are also very good for promoting evacuation. Pets enjoy them. Among those that could be used would be prunes, figs, dates, raisins, and raw apples. You can buy herbal tablets that contain a combination of cascara sagrada and aloe curacao. These are quite effective for immediate relief and can be obtained through Sonne's Organic Foods, Inc., Natick, Massachusetts 01760, or your own local store. Don't feed a constipated dog until you have relieved him. Just give distilled water and *raw* honey; then resume a diet rich in raw fruits, vegetables, sprouts, liver, milk, and whole grains. Good diet is the only sure cure for constipation.

Heart Disease

The older dog is prone to heart disease. Toxic accumulations overload the bloodstream and overtax the heart. A dog with heart problems should be detoxified by a proper diet to lessen the load on the heart. Exercise should be encouraged, for it brings oxygen to all parts of the body and improves the general circulation. Overweight also contributes to and aggravates heart problems.

A certain degree of heart ailment is evidenced in seventy to eighty percent of dogs over six or seven years. The heart may suffer inflammation, weakness, and/or valve problems. Muscular deterioration can eventually lead to a crisis response or sudden heart failure: excessive exertion or the sudden malfunction of another organ can overload the heart until it ceases to function.

The dog can become short of breath, tire easily, act generally sluggish, and cough, especially after exercise. As heart disease progresses, blood circulation and pressure are reduced sharply. Reduced oxygen causes the dog to pant as he tries to get more oxygen. Eventually he perishes from asphyxiation.

Leaky valves can be compensated for adequately by a strong heart. Heart and lungs interact, with the lungs dependant for their oxygen on a blood supply from the heart. With the aging process, the older dog loses elasticity in the lungs and arterial system. He develops hardening of the arteries, which then puts an extra load on the heart, making it very difficult to circulate blood throughout the system. When kidneys don't receive enough blood, they can't properly filter waste products from the body. The liver, being deprived of adequate blood, can no longer perform its job of detoxification. The whole body begins to be affected.

Put the dog on a good raw-food diet, with only kelp as a source of sodium and *raw* honey as a natural heart stimulant. Herbalists use rosemary leaves, dandelion leaves, and watercress. Fasting one day a week on distilled water and *raw* honey, will help to rest the digestive organs and tone up the heart muscles. Lecithin is a great natural emulsifier, to keep the arteries lower in arterial plaque. Avoid tryglycerides (the fats of sugar) that cause blood sludge and increase

51

plaque formation on arterial walls. A process that is being used successfully with humans can also be tried for dogs: it is known as chelation therapy. Chelation comes from the Latin *chela* (or claw) and chelation therapy has been used to remove toxic accumulation of lead. It acts as a roto rooter, to houseclean the arterial system. The procedure involves hooking up an intravenous drip for several hours, for a series of treatments. It is painless and has been used in humans in lieu of coronary by-pass operations. The operations are only a very elaborate and costly stop-gap measure; they do nothing to get at the cause. The cure is also that which prevents. Put your dog on a healthful diet and a good exercise program when he is young, and he very likely will not be suffering heart problems as an older dog.

Hip Dysplasia

Hip dysplasia is a common disability among the larger breeds of dogs, although it can also affect some smaller breeds. In potentially dysplastic pups of large breeds, the lack of high-strength collagen in ligaments and muscles is usually at fault. Collagen is the intracellular cement that connects tissues and gives them their strength. In turn, for good-quality collagen, the system requires ascorbate, a salt of vitamin C (ascorbic acid). Dogs produce about 40mg of ascorbate per kilogram of body weight per day, but some dogs are poor producers, among them, frequently, dogs of the larger breeds.

Accordingly, preventive programs have been set up. Pregnant bitches are fed megadoses of ascorbate, and their pups are fed it from birth to the age of two years. There has been great success with such measures.

If your dog has hip dysplasia, try the ascorbate therapy. You have nothing to lose, and your dog has everything to gain.

Chapter V

NUTRITION

Nutritional Awareness

Knowledge of nutrition is of paramount importance to the maximum health and longevity of any animal, be it human, dog, or other. What foods our animals ingest, as well as the quantity, frequency, and proper combinations of foods, will make a startling difference in the incidence of dietary-related diseases. Nutritional therapy requires acquiring a good broad-based awareness of how the body functions and what the digestive requirements are in our animal pets, in order to initiate optimum food metabolism. We should also look to what improvements we can make within the diet by various food supplements such as vitamins, minerals, and enzymes as catalytic agents or stimuli toward better and more efficient assimilation of food.

Harmful Foods and Food Additives

More and more evidence indicates that we cannot thoughtlessly yet deliberately continue to ingest foodless foods (devoid of nutritional value), refined foods (stripped of all vitamin and mineral content and then infused with highly toxic additives), enriched foods (depleted of natural food value and gratuitously sprinkled with a few spare vitamins and minerals to placate the undiscerning consumer). Every consideration you would give to building greater health for yourself would have an equal value for your animal. All animals survive best on the most natural foods possible. These foods should also be live and raw or lightly cooked wherever practicable, because high cooking heat destroys enzymatic properties in the foods that are necessary aids to digestion and to the absorption of nutrients. Heating

53

Knowledge of nutrition is of paramount importance to the health and longevity
of any animal.

can also serve to cripple or deplete vitamin and mineral activity. Animals should eat as nearly as possible in a manner that would most closely resemble their natural nutritional inclinations in the wild. Animals subsisting on the carcasses of freshly killed prey are consuming live, raw food, replete with natural vitamins, minerals, and enzymes in a highly assimilable form. This form of nutriment is also highly palatable for the animal, and it is only "civilization" that has forced the domesticated animal into harmful mockery of a good dietary regimen. In the recent past, our concept of what constitutes food has changed so drastically that we must make haste to develop a working, practical knowledge of what goes into our mouths and those of our pets, and what price we will pay for ignorance or intentional transgressions.

Toxemia

Additives, used to prolong shelf life of foods, are very often non-food substances that become stored in the body as toxic materials. These additives have a cumulative effect in the body, and do not simply pass out of the system as harmless wastes. The more toxins our animal ingests, the greater the workload on all of the endocrine organs, especially the liver and kidneys. Kidney disease is one of the most prominent causes of death in animals.

Whole Foods

In order to provide highest digestive efficiency, we must furnish the body with fuel in the form of food that can be utilized to the fullest, with the lowest storage of toxic by-products that is possible. Ideally, this should mean raw or only slightly cooked foods, without additives and preservatives, and without accompanying vitamin and mineral depletion. Food with all its own natural values provides the building blocks for the body; without adequate quality, our anatomical structures will suffer.

Sugar

Beware of pet foods that have sugar as an additive or preservative. Sugar is most widely used for these purposes, although this insidiously addictive substance has absolutely *no beneficial qualities whatsoever in its refined form*. The dehydrated, semimoist packaged pet burgers contain sugar as a preservative because sugar absorbs excess moisture. But should a stored package become moist, the dormant bacteria will become reactivated and most vigorous in the ani-

55

mal's alimentary canal. A dog with a predisposition to diabetes will have its condition considerably exacerbated if on a regular maintenance of this type of food. The pancreas is being bombarded with overwork when it is required to process large quantities of refined sugar, while at the same time trying to maintain a relatively stable blood sugar level. Sugar stress overworks the pancreas, leading to diabetes and low blood sugar. Refined white sugar deprives the body of proper protein and calcium metabolization. It is also implicated in kidney disease and mental disorders. The body requires sugar, but fruits and vegetables abound with the natural version, primary sugar, which the body—human or animal—handles very well.

Sugar is also a major cause of arteriosclerosis (atherosclerosis; hardening of the arteries). Through its fats (triglycerides), it manifests itself as atheromatous plaques, along the walls of the arteries, making what looks like a clogged sewer pipe of your pet's arterial system, and predisposing the animal to stroke. We should concern ourselves far more about *sugar and refined carbohydrates* as a source of clogged arteries than the cholesterol scare that has been working up for the last decade or two. Our bodies manufacture cholesterol in the liver, and we need a certain amount for the manufacture of adrenal hormones, but that is not true of refined sugar or other refined products. *There is absolutely no redeeming nutritional value in refined sugar, and the relative good of most other refined products is far outweighed by their relative harm.*

Carbohydrates

When we advocate no sugar or refined carbohydrates, this does not mean that you can't or shouldn't give your animal first-grade primary sources of carbohydrate energy. Whole wheat bread, toasted, not enriched but one-hundred-percent whole grain, will make a very fine carbohydrate addition to your pet's diet. (White bread is whole wheat bread before the refinement process robbed it of all nutritional value and bleached the flour with toxic substances.) The same benefit is in many seven-grain and other whole-grain breads that have all the delicious nutritional value naturally left in. There are other good sources of carbohydrates for your pet in whole-grain cereal flakes like wheat flakes, oat flakes, barley, rye, corn, rice, and millet flakes. Among the cooked cereals, wheatena, whole grits, corn meal, and oatmeal can be used. Unprocessed grains such as millet, buckwheat, barley, wheat, oats, rye, corn, and brown rice are very nutritious and palatable foods for your pet. Natural brown rice is a very good source of nutriment because it contains many of the natural food values in the hull. Polished white rice has been rubbed and scrubbed into a lifeless source of empty calories.

Remember, when dealing with your older dog, he needs high-quality food even more crucially than the younger animal. The bodily functions are beginning to show clinical symptoms of the nutritional abuse that has been dealt the heretofore healthy organs. In short, they are slowly wearing out. It is foolish to speak of the preservation of health in the older dog without also being aware of the nutritional priorities that can bring about that much-desired health and longevity.

Pure Water

Pure water is another important consideration. Water is a life-sustaining necessity, but if the water is filled with all manner of disease-producing bacteria, fungi, and harmful flora, plus chloride, fluoride, and other assorted toxic matter added in an effort to reduce its infectious qualities, then its life- and health-giving properties are indeed dubious. If a dog is in ill health, drinking distilled water can help to detoxify his system. An animal is often sick from a slow accumulation of toxins or poisons built up over the years from improper

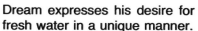
Dream expresses his desire for fresh water in a unique manner.

food and water consumption. To help make the gastrointestinal damage that may have occurred less severe, you can put your pet on distilled drinking water instead of his regular water.

Distilled water is pure H_2O, with the minerals left *out*, with no chlorine (to kill the harmful flora and fauna), no fluoride, and no heavy metal sludge, such as copper or lead from pipes, which helps to precipitate bladder and kidney stones. Distilled water does a very good job of removing debris from the system (it is also helpful in arthritis). But, just as it removes the bad, it also sweeps out with this much of the essential vitamin and mineral content in solution within the body. For that reason, when on a purification regimen with distilled water, it is advisable to replace vitamin and mineral loss with vitamin and mineral supplementation through capsules or tablets added to the food. If one were to go on a regimen of several weeks on distilled water, then a change-over to and a follow-up with a maintenance intake of spring water would be most beneficial. Spring water is pure H_2O with the minerals left *in*. Your pet need never drink tap water again. Why put such a heavy load upon the kidneys and other organs of purification when it is totally avoidable. Remember, if your steam iron's internal system can't take tap water, what makes you think your own or your pet's *can*?

Friendly Flora

Friendly Flora is not a kind old lady who lives nearby. Rather, friendly flora are the beneficial bacterial agents that are needed throughout the alimentary canal for assimilation and metabolization of food. Without enough friendly flora, food ingested becomes putrified and lodges as toxic matter throughout the system. Several factors are involved in the depletion of friendly flora. A primary cause is the shortage of hydrochloric acid in the stomach, as friendly flora are sustained best in an acid environment. The depletion of hydrochloric acid means a more alkaline environment in which the friendly flora cannot survive, much less thrive. Hydrochloric acid is the very powerful gastric juice that aids the disgestion of hard, chunky protein foods.

Contributing to the depletion of hydrochloric acid and the resultant loss of flora are both the wrong foods and wrong combinations of foods. An excess of carbohydrates, especially refined, foodless-junk carbohydrates, will promote acid loss. A means of combating the loss of flora is the use of various lactobacilli available in health food stores in pill, powder, liquid, or capsule form. *Natural* yogurt also contains

58

friendly flora (lactobacilli), but only if natural, from "live culture," and without sugary fruit additives and spoilage retardants. For quality and quantity control, the capsules, powder, etc., are preferable.

Whenever your pet is taking medication of any kind, such as antibiotics, the friendly flora are subject to excessive depletion through the potency of the drug action itself. Even plain old aspirin kills millions of friendly flora. It is advisable to increase the amount of supplemental friendly flora during the period in which medication is in use. Also, be very wary about combining more than one drug at a time. Drug interaction involves many complexities. It is much better to avoid all potentially harmful interactions by giving your pet only one medication at a time.

Enzymes and Food Combinations

The digestive organs secrete what are called enzymes to act upon food and break it down for proper assimilation into the body as vital cell builders. There are protein enzymes to act upon protein, carbohydrate enzymes to act upon carbohydrates, and fat enzymes to act upon fats. The enzymes that act upon the protein of meat are different from the enzymes that act upon the protein of nuts, or milk, or cheese, or eggs. The same holds true for the carbohydrate (sugar and starch) enzymes and the fat enzymes. Within the basic categories there exist many substrata of metabolic interaction.

When protein and starch are eaten together, the protein enzymes go to work on the protein first, leaving in abeyance the work of carbohydrate digestion. The stomach makes no provision for starch digestion. Unfortunately, while the starch is waiting to be digested it ferments, releasing toxins into the body, causing flatulence and belching and the storage of toxic waste through the very process of fermentation. The way to bring about a much more economical assimilation of foods is to feed your pet protein and starch at two separate meals. The chunks of protein, be they beef, liver, chicken, fish, etc., are not so easily digested by the body. They need a strong acid environment in the stomach to break down the bolus of meat protein. If there is not that much-needed acid environment, which means an adequate supply of hydrochloric acid, then protein digestion is seriously impeded.

The stomach can be tested for hydrochloric acid through a sampling of the gastric juices. You can also test the urine with nitrazine paper. If the pH (acid-alkali balance) is above six, or your test paper turns dark blue, you can be pretty sure that the stomach is alkaline

59

and needs hydrochloric acid. If the test paper is below six and manifests no change in the yellow color, or turns light to medium brown, then you can be reasonably sure that the hydrochloric acid in the stomach is sufficient. Should your pet need hydrochloric acid, this can be added to the diet in supplement form. Try the nitrazine test after one- and two-week intervals. You will be surprised at the quick reorientation to normal.

A similar gastronomic mistake will occur with the combining of fats like butter or gravy, or even milk, with other proteins and carbohydrates. Fat globules, when ingested with other foods, surround the other foods, making them impenetrable to the action of their own vital enzymes. Fats get enzymatic action, but the rest of the food just floats in the stomach far longer than advisable. A good rule to follow is, when in doubt don't combine. Save separate categories for different meals. Your pet is eating twice a day, so he can have the carbohydrates plus a little *raw* honey or vegetables at one meal, and the protein plus a little fresh, raw, grated vegetables at the other.

If very little water is given at mealtime, enzymatic action can be more efficient. Taking in great quantities of water with the food will serve to dilute enzymatic action and raise the pH of the stomach.

When you feed your pet too much second-hand, poor-quality protein such as cheap hamburgers; hot dogs; cold cuts; semimoist, cheap-quality, sugar-preserved dog foods; or any meats full of DES, nitrates, nitrites, aldehydes, and other assorted harmful additives, the particular pancreatic enzymes that are needed to digest the proteins become depleted sooner than necessary. Additionally, these meats have been so thoroughly cooked they no longer have live enzymes of their own. Without enough pancreatic enzymes to digest the protein, the food begins to putrefy and can lead to pancreatitis and toxemia. We can give more food but it is not being utilized. If the body can't use the nutrients, this is tantamount to not having them. The body begins to feed upon itself in order to sustain life, and the animal loses weight and muscle tone in spite of the quantity of food provided. In the case of malignant tumors, the body feeds the tumor while starving itself, so the tumor grows to robust proportions while the body shrivels like a dehydrated prune.

If you suspect ill health in your pet, don't stuff him with food, hoping that he will regain strength. You will actually be further depleting his impaired vitality. Witholding food for a day or so will cause a revitalization of the body, because the body will have a chance to fight the impairment without the continuing added burden of processing food. This applies whether the food is wholesome or second-rate, but even more strongly when it is of poor quality. Then the digestive organs are not working in the processing of food, they have an opportunity to apply themselves to the digestion of debris in the body. Fasting is nature's most perfect medicine, since the body works to rid itself of the debris, or harmful toxic matter, first, thereby effecting a most marvelous housecleaning of cells. Cells drowning in toxic waste have no room to absorb nutrients. They must first rid themselves of this obstructing waste. The process by which the body feeds upon and digests the debris is called autolysis. Some types of tumors· or cysts can enjoy resorption into the body through this gradual, natural purification process.

If you have an older dog, the chances are that through years of dietary indiscretions, his enzymes have become somewhat depleted. Whatever sturdy stock remains can be reinforced by adding pancreatic enzymes to the diet. This will serve to bolster the forces of protein, fat, and carbohydrate digestion, and you will be augmenting the metabolization of your animal's food. Pancreatic enzymes can help turn the tide of sluggish digestion, enabling the digestive process to perform with much increased efficiency. This, in concert with the friendly flora and the hydrochloric acid, will provide a most harmonious relationship within the digestive tract. The surplus enzymes can now effect a cleansing process by breaking up the toxic debris stored throughout the body. You will find that once the body needs no longer feed upon the protein in the muscular circuitry, muscular re-development will reappropriate protein in usable form throughout the system.

Calcium Deficiency
As stated elsewhere in this book, the older animal needs a lesser quantity of higher-quality protein, since through such abuses as we have enumerated here, he cannot absorb food as well from the intestinal tract. The phosphorus contained in meat tends to deplete the calcium level if taken as an excess of poor-quality protein. This can produce a negative calcium balance, meaning that your animal is losing calcium faster than he can take it in. A negative calcium balance can lead to osteoporosis, which is the thinning of bone. X rays would only show clinical evidence if there is a loss of thirty-five to forty percent of the calcium from the bone. By that time you have a pretty serious calcium depeltion. Observation has shown that periodontal disease, or bone loss of the supporting tooth structures, is one of the

earliest signs of osteoporosis. Before it becomes a critical problem, supplementation could be given in the form of calcium oratate, vitamins A and D, B complex, C, and other minerals involved in bone metabolism. In nature, when animals eat the bones of their prey, this provides an excellent source of calcium and other valuable minerals.

Multivitamins and Minerals

The older animal, especially, needs a good multivitamin preparation. This should contain all the essential vitamins, minerals, and amino acids in a protein base, *free of sugar or starch*. Vitamins need minerals to maximize their proper functions. They act as co-enzymes. Read the labels and get the highest potency of natural multivitamin-mineral preparation you can. Your vet should have supplies on hand, or suggest which ones may be most suitable for your animal. (Human preparations are often suitable.) Some are interchangeable for both dogs and cats and some have special hormones for the older animal. Some places sell cod liver oil as a source of vitamins A and D. However, if you get top-quality food for your dog, then unless your vet advises a particular supplement for specific reasons, usually a good multivitamin-mineral preparation will suffice. Quantities not needed by the body will, for the most part, simply pass out as waste. It is for us to concern ourselves more with a dearth of nutritional supplementation than with a surplus.

Basic Types of Food: Canned vs. Semimoist vs. Dry

People often ask: "What should I feed my dog to insure maximum nutritional benefits? There are so many types of foods to choose from. How can I know what is right for my pet?" The basic types of foods available for a dog are the canned all-beef and meat with ration (a blend of cereals and grains as well as meat by-products); the semimoist food (cellophane-wrapped chunked or chopped food, often with cheese food added); and the dry food, which could be in pellet or bite-size form.

To start, proper diet and nutrition are essential for your pet, to ensure proper weight maintenance, to maximize his physical well-being, and to provide maximum longevity. For a proper diet, your dog needs the correct proportional balance to proteins, carbohydrates, and fats, as do humans. To omit, or inadequately supply to your animal, any one of these basic components can cause serious dietary deficiencies and bring on the attendant nutritionally related deficiency diseases.

Beginning with the one-hundred-percent-pure-meat (no cereal) product—though your dog is a carnivore, a diet of pure meat is too rich in proteins. All-meat diets may also be too rich in fats, leading to possible obesity in your pet. It has been found that an all-meat diet, devoid of essential carbohydrates and bulk, can produce skin eruptions, can sometimes cause fatal inflammation of fatty tissues and increases in cholesterol and blood-urea nitrogen. Other risk factors in the all-meat diet are that often the meats are DES-impregnated (DES, diethylstilbestrol, having been used to fatten cattle prematurely and unnaturally). Diethylstilbestrol, a female hormone (estrogen; also produced synthetically), has a very clear link with cancer. When injected into women to prevent miscarriage, it has produced a fatal genital cancer in a disturbing number of offspring. Too, the nitrates and nitrites added to the meats are known to link with amines in the body to form nitrosamines, cancer-causing substances, when combined with other properties in the alimentary canal.

Fish can be a useful source of protein for dogs. It is only our own preconditioning that limits us to think of fish as cat food and beef as dog food. How many of us think of birds as carnivores? Yet they do eat the flesh of fresh worms and insects, as well as the more familiar seeds.

The recommended proportions of meat to carbohydrates and fats is approximately one-third meat to two-thirds of fat, whole grains, and other assorted nutrients, including vegetables and herbs. This would indicate that the ration food is a more balanced diet for your dog. The grains and cereals are very palatable and, as the source of carbohydrates, they provide essential energy and bulk. Bulk or fiber is needed to form stools.

Semimoist foods are convenience foods that don't require can openers or refrigeration. However they do contain large amounts of sugar, some up to twenty-five percent. You can judge the approximate amount of sugar by its position on the list of ingredients on the package. If sugar is among the first few ingredients in a product, you can be sure there is an extremely high quantity of it. Sugar is our largest food additive, and in this case it is used to absorb excess moisture, which helps keep down bacterial growth. But if the package should accidently become wet, the microorganisms can grow at an alarming rate. Canned food is heated to a level that destroys bacteria and microrganisms. Semimoist food is not, and so sugar is used to compensate for complete sterilization. Semimoist food has far less water content than canned food, and your pet will tend to supplement this deficiency with very large quantitites of water, causing frequent urination and increased housebreaking problems. The very high empty-caloric value of semimoist foods can cause your pet to acquire undesirable excess weight. Refined sugar is an addictive food that your pet can very well do without. Your dog is compelled to overeat in order to tap the few available nutrients in the food. And sugar produces a condition commonly known as blood sludge: the triglycerides, which represent the fats of sugars, can produce atheromatous plaques (arteriosclerosis).

Dry meal or kibble is a good addition to an all-meat or ration diet, but when used as the sole source of nutrition it can sometimes produce problems. Dry meal has the lowest water content of all the food types, and so more extra water will be consumed. Hence greater frequency of urination—a housebreaking problem with the puppy; a general urinary problem in the older dog. Your pet may also need a supplement of corn oil, or perhaps wheat germ oil, since there is generally not enough fat in this type of food. Lacking fat, the dog could develop dry, itching, and flaking skin; dandruff, sparse hair, etc. Also, since this food is only ten percent water, if water is not mixed into this food, your dog can wolf down large amounts of dry food and then drink a tremendous quantity of water. This will cause the food to expand in the dog's stomach, uncomfortably causing intestinal bloat and possibly gastric torsion. The latter condition, common in larger breeds, can be fatal. The dog gets a pocket of gas that he is unable to expell. He swells like a balloon and, unless excess gas can be absorbed by charcoal tablets or some other means, your pet can have an untimely death. His stomach can flip over, literally closing off the passageway at both ends. Prompt surgical procedures are often required to remedy this condition.

Now that we have possibly scared you into throwing out all of Fido's food, let's discuss what could be fed from among the commercially available preparations. We would suggest a canned ration mixture (making a check to see if the can has the seal of continuous inspection by the U.S. Department of Agriculture. This service is paid for by the manufacturer, and should insure meat by-products that would even be safe for human consumption.) Other sources may have what is known as 4-D by-products, meaning meat from dead, dying, diseased, or disabled animals, which are considered unfit for human consumption. In making your choice, try to select foods with as few additives and preservatives as possible. It costs about twelve cents to pack a can of plain water and some dog foods are selling for sixteen cents a can. What quality food could possibly be in that can for the four-cent nutrition investment?

To round out the menu, equal portions of some dry pellets or kibble food should be added to the canned ration. Mix it in well with the ration, to allow partial expansion to take place in the bowl instead of all in the dog's stomach. Always have water on hand, except forty-five minutes before and forty-five minutes after eating, so as not to dilute enzymatic action and disturb the proper pH of the stomach. Feed your animal twice a day, once in the morning and again in late afternoon if possible. An older dog can even go back to three meals a day. The ration provides all the fats, proteins, and carbohydrates in a moist, palatable form, while the dry food reduces tartar formation on the teeth, improves intestinal motility, and is enjoyably crunchy for your dog. If you can get slow-baked kibble rather than extruded puffs of questionable value, you will have more retained nutritive value. Expect to pay more for the slow-baked product, but you will be feeding much less and satisfying your dog's hunger with a maximum assimilation of nutrients and the minimum residue of fecal waste.

Healthful Additions to Commercial Foods

When you choose commercially prepared pet foods, try to get the best quality you can, free of, or low in, additives. In addition to your commercial preparation, or combination of them, there is every reason to include, also, some very finely chopped vegetables, such as carrots and/or carrot tops, parsley, celery and/or celery tops, peppers, or any other variety of greens, and sprouts (lentil, mung, or alfalfa) to your pet's menu. These can be mixed in with the regular meal, and should be raw for maximum benefits of vitamins, minerals, and live enzymes. Vegetables can be wonderful natural sources of protein, starch, sugars, and fat, and in one deliciously assimilable form. A little *raw, unpasteurized,* honey may be added to some spring water or used on cereal or toast, on a regular basis or especially when you suspect bacterial upset in the animal's stomach. Raw honey has been shown to have antibacterial properties and, besides, is an excellent source of natural primary sugar that the body can easily absorb and use.

Mucus plays a significant role in clogging the entire alimentary canal, impairing digestion and preventing the absorption of nutrients. Heavy mucus formation seriously inhibits the peristaltic action of the alimentary canal, which is the wavelike muscle spasms that propel and assist the food in moving along the digestive tract. Mucus forms when we feed our pets too many foods that can produce it, such as milk, meats, cheeses, fats, and carbohydrates. Obviously these foods are good—in balanced proportion—but an excess of them is not. Mucus-lean and mucusless foods are the fruits and vegetables. Beyond their already-discussed nutritional values, their addition to the diet, raw, but grated for easy assimilation, lies in their mucus-cleaning or mucus-mitigating properties. Vegetables and fruits are nature's brooms, as is bran (a great regulator), and they effect a natural housecleaning of the alimentary canal. They clean the system of mucous sludge, toxic and decaying matter, and help to prevent diverticulosis.

Garlic is another of nature's brooms, helping to reduce mucus in the intestines. Garlic has been touted for years as a means to ward off worms and intestinal parasites, and this is not a "quack" superstition. There is sound nutritional methodology here. By reducing intestinal mucus, a breeding ground for worms is removed. Worms and other parasites prey on filth. Remove the ambiance in which they thrive, and they must perish. This is why many natural-rearing breeders will put a clove or more of fresh garlic daily into their animals' meat ration. They have found that the addition of fresh garlic helps keep the colon mucus-lean; releases sulfur to the skin's surface, to ward off fleas; reduces blood pressure; detoxifies the body; and keeps the animals in better health generally.

If your dog's menu needs changing, do it gradually over a period of a few days to a week. Don't concern yourself if your pet holds out, even for a few days. Just continue feeding him what is healthful, even if not what he likes, and your animal will be both happier and healthier for it. Healthful foods; good diet supplements; a competent, understanding vet; and a loving and stable home life will go a long way in promoting health and happiness in the older dog, thereby making his life as rich and rewarding as it really can be.

CORRECT FOOD COMBINING

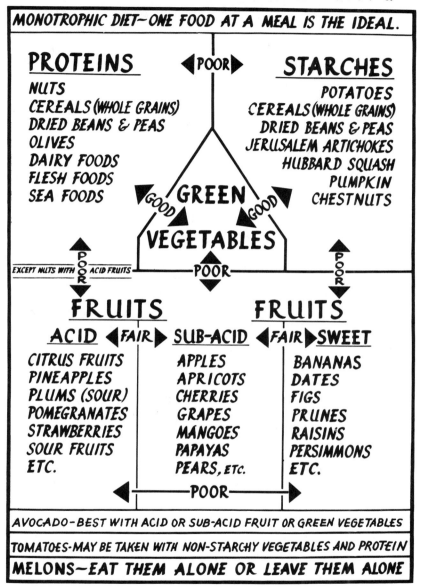

MONOTROPHIC DIET—ONE FOOD AT A MEAL IS THE IDEAL.

PROTEINS ◀POOR▶ **STARCHES**

NUTS
CEREALS (WHOLE GRAINS)
DRIED BEANS & PEAS
OLIVES
DAIRY FOODS
FLESH FOODS
SEA FOODS

POTATOES
CEREALS (WHOLE GRAINS)
DRIED BEANS & PEAS
JERUSALEM ARTICHOKES
HUBBARD SQUASH
PUMPKIN
CHESTNUTS

GOOD ▶ **GREEN** ◀ GOOD

VEGETABLES

POOR

EXCEPT NUTS WITH POOR ACID FRUITS

POOR

FRUITS   **FRUITS**

ACID ◀FAIR▶ SUB-ACID ◀FAIR▶ SWEET

CITRUS FRUITS
PINEAPPLES
PLUMS (SOUR)
POMEGRANATES
STRAWBERRIES
SOUR FRUITS
ETC.

APPLES
APRICOTS
CHERRIES
GRAPES
MANGOES
PAPAYAS
PEARS, ETC.

BANANAS
DATES
FIGS
PRUNES
RAISINS
PERSIMMONS
ETC.

◀—POOR—▶

AVOCADO—BEST WITH ACID OR SUB-ACID FRUIT OR GREEN VEGETABLES

TOMATOES-MAY BE TAKEN WITH NON-STARCHY VEGETABLES AND PROTEIN

MELONS—EAT THEM ALONE OR LEAVE THEM ALONE

A healthful diet is essential, especially for the older dog.

Chapter VI

PREVENTIVE MEDICINE AT ANY AGE

Importance of Good Diet

We cannot impress upon you too strongly how essential a healthful diet is, especially for the older dog. Every degenerative disease your older dog suffers, be it heart problems, arthritis, cancer, kidney failure, or cataracts, is in some way related to nutritional deficiencies or to poor absorption of nutrients.

Most authorities agree that the older dog needs more vitamin and mineral supplementation, as well as a smaller quantity of higher-quality food (higher biological value). Many of the experts, however, do not properly interpret degenerative symptoms into recognition of substandard nutrition. Very few dog books deal really comprehensively with the subject of nutrition. When your dog is young, time is on his side, even considering the numerous nutritional errors visited upon him in his daily menu. But, who is to blame? Does your dog know or care that he is not getting optimum nourishment? No! Do you, his owner, realize that many of the old dog's ills are occurring far too early and essentially are preventable through proper nutrition? No!

Toxemia and the Colon

So there's the rub. We can only try here and now to have you realize that essentially there is only one canine disease; *toxemia*. By whatever local disease names or manifestations you choose to call it, waste matter is backing up in the cells of the body and causing them to malfunction or to cease functioning. How do our animals get into this shameful condition? The shocking truth is that most often they eat the wrong foods.

Autopsies are routinely performed on dogs that have died of some mysterious insult to their beings, but rarely does it occur to the practitioner that the source of the ill could lie in putrefaction in the colon. The large intestine (colon) develops rings of fecal waste, much like a tree acquires rings as it advances in age. The rings gradually solidify into impermeable yellow plaster (fecal matter) that becomes quite hard. These layers of fecal plaster impair a very obvious function. The main mode of movement of food from the esophagus to the rectum is peristalsis, the wavelike motion used by the digestive system to push the food from one end of the body to the other. A dog's colon is normally an efficient sewage system for the evacuation of wastes. But we have, in all innocence, turned it into a cesspool of seething putrefaction. Without peristalsis, fecal matter continues to collect in the colon. Without proper elimination, disease-producing bacteria increase in the intestines. With the intestines stuccoed with dried fecal matter, how can good food be absorbed through the walls of the intestines? What is to prevent contamination of good nutrients by putrefactive juices? The ileocecal valve, the flexure that acts to push food from the small to large intestine, is often draped in feces. So it either jams open, or it jams shut; either way, your dog has trouble.

Seeking a Natural Dog Food

In the hopes that your older dog can enjoy a Golden Age that you never thought possible, we would like to explore the evolvement of a nutritionally wholesome, additive-free, all-natural dog food. The rewards of such a monumental endeavor would be great. If successful, there would be a constant improvement in the overall health of animals fed on such a natural diet. Specific benefits need not be listed: they would include amelioration of almost every disease and condition affected by nutritional deficiencies. Food is a highly significant factor in the viability of your pet's health. Doctors who are nutritionally oriented know that most all the medications with fancy trade and generic names are primarily palliatives for disease symptoms that the body must ultimately fight off itself.

So the important questions become what factors have caused or contributed to particular disease conditions and how they can best be removed. What are the considerations involved in developing a natural dog food and how do you assess the ingredients already in the pet food of your choice? With this knowledge you will be capable of choosing wisely and of upgrading any pet food nutritionally.

Sugar

We have already discussed refined sugar in the previous chapter. In sugar cane or in sugar beets the juices are a complete and wholesome food, but as we normally see the end product, its nutrients extracted, it is a lifeless product capable of great harm both to pets and to their masters. In lists of product ingredients, sugar is frequently listed (disguised) as sucrose, dextrose, etc. Any ingredient that ends in "ose" should be suspect.

Proteins; Fats; Carbohydrates

The broadest food classifications are proteins, fats, and carbohydrates. They aid us in assessing the major components of a food. Foods are generally considered to be of the category that predominates in their composition. But this does not mean that a carbohydrate such as wheat contains no protein—it does. Or that a protein such as liver contains no carbohydrates—it does. Pets, like people, need a proper ratio of proteins, fats, and carbohydrates to maintain proper health.

Proteins are vital to the growth and development of all body tissues. Protein aids in the formation of hormones; it regulates the acid-alkaline and water balances; and it helps the body to form enzymes and antibodies. Protein also aids in the formation of milk during lactation, and in the process of blood clotting. Protein can be used as an energy source when fats and carbohydrates are insufficient in the diet.

Fats (lipids) are the most concentrated energy source in the diet. When oxidized, fats yield more than twice the calories of proteins or carbohydrates. Fats act as carriers for the fat-soluble vitamins A, D, E, and K. By helping vitamin D to be absorbed, fats make calcium more available to body tissues. Fats also aid in the conversion of carotene to vitamin A. Fats insulate major organs such as the heart, liver, and kidneys, and help to maintain body heat.

Carbohydrates are the major source of energy for all bodily functions. They are a splendid source of *quick* energy. They assist in the digestion of other foods, and they are essential in regulating protein and fat metabolism. Carbohydrates are considered the fuel in which the fat burns. Carbohydrates consist of sugars, starches, and cellulose. Simple sugars, as in honey and fruits, are easily digested. Starches, however, require extensive enzymatic action. All starches and sugars are converted to glucose or blood sugar, which then is used as fuel by tissues of the brain, nervous system, and muscles. Carbohydrates can be synthesized in the body from amino acids and the glycerol component of fats, but if the body does not get enough from an outside source it will break down body protein as a source of energy.

Chemical Additives

Natural foods, today, are understood to contain no artificial or synthetic additives to preserve flavor, sweeten, color, or in any other way enhance the natural properties of the foods. This applies especially to nonfood substances. Yet it is particularly chemical, nonfood additives that are the most common—primarily to add shelf life and to improve appearance, regardless of the cumulative effect they may have upon your pet. There are literally thousands of additives, but the five that head the list should suffice to make our point.

Sodium nitrate and sodium nitrite are chemical preservatives and color fixatives. In both humans and pets they are capable of inducing cancer, mutations, and monster-growths. Sodium nitrate converts readily to sodium nitrite (the more toxic), and the nitrite has produced severe arthritic symptoms, epileptic-like changes in brain activity, and decreased liver storage of vitamin A and carotene, inducing deficiency symptoms, all in laboratory animals. The toxicity of nitrites comes from their ability to disable hemoglobin, the molecule in red blood cells that carries life-giving oxygen. Nitrites are one of the few food additives that are definitely known to have caused deaths in the United States.

Monosodium glutamate (MSG) serves no purpose except to heighten food flavors or to suppress or disguise the flavors of inferior or damaged foods. MSG has been put into animal feeds (cattle, swine, poultry, and sheep) since it induces them to eat more. It suppresses oxidized flavors that may develop during storage. Passed through the food chain to humans or pets, or as added directly to prepared foods, MSG can cause bloating and distention, belching, numbness and general weakness, palpitation, cold sweat, and viselike throbbing in the head. Laboratory experiments on mice have revealed brain damage, nerve-cell death, stunted skeletal development, marked obesity, and female sterility, showing that effects are more than transitory. MSG is a most concentrated source of sodium, to the extent that a few years ago, as the result of a public outrage, one of the largest packers of baby foods removed it completely from its products.

droxyanisole) are another fine pair of preservatives. BHT, the more toxic, was originally developed to prevent color film from deteriorating, and the safety testing of both products was done by the industry desiring to market products with these additives, rather than by any independent research source. BHT, in experiments and controlled studies, has demonstrated damaging effects including metabolic stress, suppression of the growth rate, loss of overall weight while increasing liver weight, other liver damage, increase of serum cholesterol, baldness, and fetal abnormalities. BHT has caused tingling sensations in face and hands, weakness, fatigue, chest tightness and difficulty in breathing, and severe allergies. BHA has retarded growth in young laboratory animals and has caused weight loss in adult animals. Both chemicals are used as antioxidants. BHT has been banned both in Sweden and Australia; Great Britain has banned its use in baby foods and cut to half its use in other foodstuffs.

Look at the labels on your pet's foods. Anything that is not readily recognized should be suspect. Change brands when you question the safety of ingredients in any food. Write to manufacturers and ask them to find alternatives to the toxic chemicals they now put in pet foods. If everybody does his share, we can effect a broad change on the manufacturing as well as the marketing level. An educated buyer is your pet's best friend.

Since dogs don't see in color, it is not for our pets that their food' is colored with the harmful additives nitrates and nitrites. The federal government wisely prohibits the use of a known carcinogenic agent in food, but what happens after a substance leaves the container and enters the body? Nitrates and nitrites combine with amines in the body to form nitrosamines, known cancer-causing agents. But because the cancer isn't gestating in the can or other container, the superpowers are absolved of all responsibility for the potential insidious end result.

Fillers

Animal food can contain all manner of nonnutritive fillers such as chicken feathers; horse and cattle hair; dehydrated, degreased garbage; peanut hulls; newspaper; dried poultry waste and other fecal matter; and decomposed leather meal. Fillers like some of the above will boost the crude analysis of the protein, but leave much to be desired insofar as nourishing the dog is concerned.

Digestibility

When looking on a pet food package, the label will have a

guaranteed crude analysis. It will then list proteins, fats, fiber, and moisture, with a minimum or maximum percentage for each. These figures are essentially meaningless since we have no way of knowing how digestible each category is, or what the biological value is of the composite food. Protein and fats are self-explanatory, whereas fiber means nonnutritive bulk or roughage, and moisture means water. When you add all these figures together and subtract from one hundred, you then have the carbohydrate percentage. Here again the figure means nothing unless you know what form the carbohydrate is in and how digestible it is.

Digestibility means what is getting to the animal at the cell level, what is being metabolized and assimilated to actually nourish the body. Many people may take it for granted that any food will nourish an animal. This is no more true with animals than it would be with people. A hoard of foods on the market provide "empty calories." But the body does not just eliminate foodless foods with no adverse consequences. Many inferior foods put stress on the body's hormonal balance and enzyme system, storing toxins in the tissues, organs, and bones. These toxins later can break out as diseases, diseases that run the gamut from colds to cancer. So, in the interest of health management, digestibility becomes a very important factor.

Foods that are closest to nature, minimally processed and complete, would be those with the greatest inherent digestibility. Live enzymes and unadulterated natural vitamins and minerals provide less stress on the organs of digestion and allow for more complete absorption.

Biological Value

One way to qualitatively measure a given food is to know its biological value. Dr. Donald Collins, in his excellent book *The Collins Guide To Dog Nutrition*, categorizes a protein by the completeness of its essential amino acids content. Essential means the body cannot manufacture them and the food must provide them. Proteins are broken down into amino acids and there are ten known essential amino acids for dogs; the other thirteen amino acids can be manufactured inside the animal's body. Eggs have the highest biological value, that of 100, for they contain all ten essential amino acids in proper proportion for the body's needs. Horsemeat protein has a biological value of 87, soy protein a biological value of 68, milk a biological value in the high 80s, cottage cheese and fish also approximate that of horsemeat. Proteins having biological values below 60 will not supply enough amino acids to meet an animal's minimum daily requirement (MDR) no matter how much is fed. If a protein has to be used for energy, this will decrease its biological value. That is why it is important to obtain energy from fat and carbohydrate sources. Proteins containing the largest number of essential amino acids yield the greatest biological value to the animal. The dog's protein requirements will depend partly upon how well that protein can supply all of his essential amino acids in the proper ratio.

The biological value of fats is assessed in a slightly different way. Fats are judged by their ability to furnish calories and essential fatty acids to an animal. Calories plus essential fatty acids equal energy, although energy is generally considered as measured in calories alone. The most important essential unsaturated fatty acid for the animal is linoleic acid. Linolenic and arachidonic acids are also considered essential, but these can be synthesized in a dog's body from linoleic if there is enough in the diet. Poultry fat is very high in linoleic acid, which means poultry fat has a high biological value, thereby being extremely valuable to the animal.

Vitamin F

Linoleic acid and all the essential unsaturated fatty acids are known collectively as vitamin F. Unsaturated fatty acids work in concert with saturated fatty acids. Cholesterol is kept soft in part by the unsaturated fatty acids, which reduce the possibilities of developing severe atherosclerosis. Animal owners are concerned with the benefits of linoleic acid in keeping the coat from drying out, the skin from flaking, the hairs from shedding. Unsaturated fatty acids aid in the transportation of oxygen to cells, tissues, and organs. Vitamin F also lubricates cells, combining with protein and cholesterol to form living membranes that hold body cells together. Vitamin F regulates blood coagulation and breaks up cholesterol buildup on arterial walls. It regulates glandular activity, especially that of the adrenals and thyroid; it maintains healthy mucous membranes and nerves. It also aids vitamin D in making calcium and phosphorus available to tissues, and helps the conversion of carotene into vitamin A. Vitamin F maintains the normal functioning of the reproductive system. Foods abundant in vitamin F are wheat germ, seeds, crude unrefined oils, and cod liver oil.

Caloric Density

Pet foods should be formulated to have a greater caloric density.

This signifies a greater concentration of calories per pound of food than would be found in a cheap filler-type pet food. For the ecology-minded individual, that means less fecal waste. If your animal can satisfy his caloric requirements with smaller amounts of higher-quality food, there is no need to load up on a lot of useless bulk. Some bulk is necessary for intestinal motility and for the cleanliness of the colon, but too much bulk can lead to a full feeling, devoid of nutritive value. This can lead to subsequent faulty absorption of nutrients and all the horrors described in the early part of this chapter under *Toxemia*. By feeding your dog a high-biological-value, high-digestibility, high-caloric-density food you are better insuring the health of the colon, as well as that of the entire body. Mounds of feces do not indicate a healthy pet. What this does indicate is that the food eaten is of low digestibility, high volume, and low caloric density.

To Salt or Not to Salt?

When looking at the ingredients on a package of pet food, you will almost invariably come upon the universal ingredient—salt, which means iodized salt. To salt or not to salt, that is the question. The body needs sodium, and the body needs iodine, but does the body need sodium chloride? Many nutritionists think not. When we check the amount of sodium naturally occurring in the body, we find the body has only one percent. Yet the body has three parts sodium to one part potassium. In sodium chloride there is the alarming ratio of about 10,000 to 1 in favor of sodium, with almost as high a ration in sea salt.

Sodium chloride (NaCl) is very controversial and its risks are many. Natural sodium occurs in vegetables such as celery, spinach, beets, and carrots. Low-sodium diets are prescribed to relieve kidney problems and hypertension. Overconsumption of salt constricts the blood vessels, forcing the heart to pump harder to get a little blood through strangled capillaries. Salt draws water out of blood cells and vessels, leading to dehydration and shrinkage of tissues. Kidneys trapped with salt can lead to edema (swelling) and a generally bloated appearance.

Sea salt is nutritionally preferable to rock salt because sea salt is higher in trace minerals such as silicon, copper, calcium, and nickel. Refined salt is heated to 1200° F and then flash cooled. Refined salt, with the exception of kosher salt, is also combined with multiple additives. Potassium iodide is used as a source of iodine, for antigoiter factors. Iodine, however, oxidizes rapidly when exposed to light, so dextrose is added as a stabilizer. These two additives would turn the salt purple, so sodium bicarbonate is used as a bleach. Then the free-flowing feature is obtained by adding sodium silicoaluminate, and we have finally arrived at the "when it rains, it pours" status. But note all the *extra* sodium compounds. The body is being pickled in salt if there is an excessive consumption. Calcium carbonate is a natural compound that can be added to natural salts to prevent caking. Natural salts contain no iodine because of their volatile oxidation properties when exposed to light. If salt could be harvested, dried, stored, and consumed in absolute darkness, then you would have naturally occuring iodine in your sea and rock salt. Since this is not feasible, we add synthetic iodine in the form of potassium iodide, as mentioned before.

The iodine in iodized salt has a low bioavailability, so what about the thyroid? Seaweeds called kelp offer a very interesting alternative. First, the ratio of sodium to potassium in kelp is only about 5 to 1, much closer to the body's own natural ratio. Secondly, kelp is a rich source of readily available iodine and of many needed trace minerals. So let us examine its other properties, as against the hazards of iodized salt.

The Alternative: Kelp

Kelp is a sea vegetable with naturally occurring iodine stabilized by the plant's own complex sugars. The amount of iodine would vary according to the locality, as well as the time of year. Kelp contains more minerals and vitamins than many highly touted health foods. It is used for obesity, for goiter problems, and for digestive problems. Kelp acts as a great thryroid regulator and provides the perfectly natural source of all the iodine we normally require. Iodine, as it naturally occurs in kelp, will relieve nervous tension and increase mental concentration through the increased free flow of blood to the brain. Kelp increases the function of the parathyroids, regulators of calcium, iodine, and sodium, which all contribute to the health and elasticity of the arterial walls. Kelp helps to remove arterial plaque and maintain tone in the blood-vessel walls. Kelp is NOT contraindicated while using any other medicine. There are few, if any, of the internal organs that kelp does not aid, from the pylorus to the prostate gland or the uterus, and including the liver, the gall bladder, the pancreas, the bile duct, the kidneys, and the colon itself.

Additionally, as an ointment for cuts, sores, boils, and pimples, kelp can be mixed with petroleum jelly in the proportions of one teaspoon kelp to two ounces of jelly. Seaweed is a natural food for dogs, often found in the stomach contents of their prey in the wilds. Seaweed contributes dark pigment to eyes, nose, and claws. It also stimulates hair growth and strong bones.

With a realistic and comprehensive comparison between iodized salt and kelp, it is up to you to decide which you favor for your own dog's diet.

Oils and Fats

Do you know what oil to buy as supplementation to your pet's diet, and do you know if there is enough oil in the pet food of your choice or if it is of the proper quality? Pet food manufacturers sometimes advertise "complete and balanced" on their pet food labels. They imply, even sometimes state explicitly, that all your dog will ever need is Brand XYZ and his well-being is ensured. But is this the case? The very process of heating a food for commercial purposes destroys many vital factors in the food, including enzymes, vitamins, and oils. Heating alters the composition of a natural oil. This unavoidable modification of its original properties frequently decreases the nourishment we seek for our pets.

A big commercial issue is that of saturated versus unsaturated fats (or oils). Saturated fats are those that become solid at room temperature. Examples are bacon or pork fat (lard), beef or lamb fat (suet or tallow), poultry fat, and milk fat (butter). Saturated fats are most often associated with animal products. Unsaturated fats are those that remain liquid at room temperature. Among them are corn oil, olive oil, peanut oil, soy, sesame, sunflower, safflower, and wheat germ oils. Most unsaturated fats are derived from seeds, nuts, and grains as indicated by those mentioned above. For a few exceptions, cottonseed oil, while widely used in foodstuffs, sometimes is not considered a food product since cotton is not a food. Also, coconut oil is considered to be a saturated fat even though it is liquid at room temperature.

It is not necessary here to go into the processing of oils from the nuts, grains, seeds, etc. The purer the oil—the less refined—the more expensive it is. The more refining—the more heat or the more of chemical extraction—the less nutritive it is and the more subject to rancidity. Processing has robbed all the naturally occurring antioxidants so, to prevent rancidity, preservatives are added. It is, once again, the usual commercial cycle.

78

The very nature of the commercial cycle precludes the likelihood of finding a good food oil prepared for pets. What you can get is a high-biological-value fat, such as poultry fat, to add to natural pet foods of low fat content. Or visit your health food store and buy a crude, unrefined oil such as corn, peanut, olive, wheat germ, or safflower. Add the oil into the daily ration, at from half a teaspoonful to a tablespoonful, depending upon the size of your dog, for supplementation of unsaturated fatty acids. Do it for the love of your pet. Also, be sure the fat in your regular pet foods is not preserved with BHA or BHT.

Alfalfa

It is important to provide a natural source of multiminerals for our pets, and there are numerous ways of doing this. We spoke of kelp as being the finest natural source of iodine, as well as a potent source of multiminerals. The second choice for naturally occurring multiminerals in a pet food would be alfalfa, truly one of nature's finest seeds. The roots of the alfalfa plant run very deep into the soil, thereby picking up many valuable minerals; it has ten times the mineral value of most grains. The organic minerals it contains are those most readily used by the body: phosphorus, silicon, aluminum, calcium, magnesium, sulphur, sodium, and potassium in just the proper proportions to build bones, teeth, nerves, and muscles; maintain a stable heartbeat, healthy organs, good posture, and an alert mind. Alfalfa is put into the better pet foods, and its inclusion indicates some nutritional forethought. It is more expensive than cheap filler substances, but not so prohibitive as to be economically impracticable. Of all the seeds, alfalfa is also the richest source of vitamin C and chlorophyll. (The advantages of chlorophyll are numerous. It helps to build hemoglobin, acts as a general detoxifier, cuts catarrh (mucus) from the system, and helps to overcome radiation effects on the body.) An important thing to remember is that vitamins need minerals as co-enzymes to work efficiently. Sparing the small cost of minerals in a pet food preparation is truly a misplaced economy and a grievous error. If your chosen pet food contains alfalfa, your dog is one step closer to optimum health.

Cereal Grains

Cereal grains are very important sources of essential minerals and vitamins, as well as of carbohydrates. *Whole* grains are of great nutritional potential in a natural pet food. If your chosen pet food doesn't contain some of the grains, there is no reason you cannot add them yourself, thereby customizing your very own product.

Pet foods most often contain corn in some form, be it whole corn, corn meal, or corn flour. Corn is a very reliable source of carbohydrates. It is inexpensive, always available, and very high in vitamin E, linoleic acid, and lecithin. Corn meal is high in magnesium, needed for good bowel function. Fresh young corn is quite desirable, grated right off the cob and eaten raw, mixed with milk. Fresh corn eaten this way is very sweet and it contains the vital germ, bran, and all essential nutrients intact. For pets, corn could be stripped off the cob and added to their ration. However, corn, also referred to as maize, can be found in pet foods in a number of forms. Corn flour usually has only the endosperm, which is the starchy portion. Whole ground corn, or cornmeal, would be preferable. Corn is vital for fertility, sound teeth, and abundant hair.

Corn flour is analogous to refined white flour for its general lack of nutritional value. Corn flour, like white flour, has been denatured, with its bran and germ essentially removed, leaving only the starchy endosperm. Your pet can do well without this fractured version of corn. Conversely, whole ground corn is a very fine food. Usually a hammer mill is used and all the vital nutrients remain substantially intact.

Barley is one of the earliest grains known, dating to thousands of years before Christ. It is very high in calcium and magnesium, and also in sodium. It generates extreme heat in the body, thereby building up a certain amount of fat. Unpearled barley should be used; it makes a good breakfast cereal for your pet, together with some raw sprouts or other grated raw vegetables. It is the most alkaline cereal, cleansing and cooling the blood in hot weather. Barley cultivates nerves and muscles, is much easier to digest than wheat, stimulates the nerves, and is helpful in keeping the body limber. Barley does not form gas, and so it is good for pets with problem digestion. It can be used as an external poultice for skin problems, and barley water is used in kidney diseases.

Buckwheat (kasha) is a very soft grain, rich in minerals and vitamins, especially the B complex, including B17, and E. Buckwheat is very high in rutin, the bioflavanoid that helps build capillary strength and arterial walls; which, in turn, reduces blood pressure and varicose veins. Buckwheat is not usually found in pet foods, but you can whip it up in no time as an alternative breakfast cereal, or use it together with barley or many of the other whole grains.

Millet is another ancient grain. It has the smallest seed and the highest potency within the grain family of the nitrilosides (vitamin B17). It is a staple in the diet of the Hunzas, essentially a cancer-free race of people, considered by some to be the world's healthiest race. Millet has been assessed as a complete food, high in protein (good amino acid balance), high in minerals, calcium, riboflavin, and lecithin. **Eight ounces of millet contain almost 23 grams of protein.** Millet is alkaline-forming and readily digestible. It provides excellent supplementation for an allergic animal and does not form alcohol after stomach digestion as do wheat, rye, and other acid grains.

Oats are a very good muscle builder, a good source of iron, and an intestinal cleanser. They are a vital food for studs and bitches. Oats don't have as much gluten as wheat. They are a less allergenic grain and contain some nitrilosides. Oats are also high in silicon, which helps the development of the muscles, brain, and nerve structures. Flaked whole oatmeal can be soaked raw overnight in a little raw milk, and then served to your pet for breakfast. Oats are a grain that can be found in the better pet foods, but try to determine if they are whole oats or oat flour that may have been degerminated.

Rice is a fine grain for animals, but it should only be unpolished brown rice. Brown rice contains vitamin B, phosphorus, potassium, magnesium, sodium, calcium, and silicon. Rice is well known for its ability to cure dysentery. It also helps build strong bones and teeth. Pet foods will not generally contain whole brown rice; if present, it may be listed as ground whole brown rice. So this is another substance with which you could occasionally augment your pet's diet. If only white rice is available, you can add wheat bran to augment vitamins and provide roughage.

Rye is another whole grain that would rarely turn up in pet foods. If it does, it would be listed as either rye mill run or rye middlings. Rye is rich in vitamin E, phosphorus, magnesium, silicon, and unsaturated fatty acids (vitamin F). It also contains fluorine. Rye is low in carbohydrates and fats, and so can be fed to obese dogs. You can get rye cereal in a health food store and cook it up with a variety of other grains or by itself. There is also available a seven-grain cereal that would provide excellent nutrition for your pet, since he would be gaining the multiple benefits of many grains.

Wheat is the most popular and most heavily consumed of all the grains, and it has the highest gluten content. Gluten is the protein of the wheat. Wheat is a product that builds fat, and if used to the exclusion of all other grains, it can cause acidosis (a harmful condition in which the blood and tissues are less alkaline than normal). Whole wheat is still an excellent grain, providing a rich source of protein, minerals, and vitamin E. Wheat germ (raw) is one of the finest sources of vitamin E, and it can be added as a daily ration to your pet's food. Many commercial foods will have wheat products listed among their ingredients. However, you don't want wheat flour, which is partially refined; look for 100-percent whole wheat meal. Many pet foods will have wheat germ meal, but the vitamin E is lost in the high heating process. For this reason it is wise to supplement with raw wheat germ. You may also add wheat bran as a source of dietary fiber.

Food-Induced Hypersensitivities

Among the flesh foods, beef and beef by-products are probably the most allergenic (capable of causing allergies), followed by horse-meat, pork, fish, chicken, chicken by-products, mutton, and lamb. Wheat and corn are among the most allergenic of the grains. This consideration is very important for animals who suffer food-induced hypersensitivities. In looking for a natural pet food, we must further refine our selections in terms of trying to avoid the most common allergy-producing foods.

Alfred Plechner, a DVM from California, has made an extensive study of food-induced hypersensitivity. He believes that about 35 percent of all hypersensitivity in our canine and feline pets is food induced. Dr. Plechner believes food-induced hypersensitivity can affect animals as young as one month old, which suggests a genetic predisposition. Often the FIH manifests after the immune system is repeatedly exposed to the offending antigen. (An antigen is any substance that stimulates the formation of antibodies when introduced into the system. An antibody, in turn, develops to counteract the antigen or allergy-producing substance.) So, traditional all-beef diets would be more antigenic than less conventional new foods, although the animal can also become sensitive to a new food over a period of repeated exposure. It takes only a minute amount of antigen in a highly sensitized patient to elicit a reaction. Some animals can tolerate − 3 grams of the offending food, whereas 4 grams will cause open reaction. Many animal patients react unfavorably to dry foods with a high antigenic protein and grain level. Dr. Plechner feels that a nonantigenic diet would consist of perhaps soymeal, brown rice, carrots, celery, garlic, and water. These choices can, of course, be made when formulating a natural pet food.

The indications of FIH are many. Among them are gastroenteritis, dermatitis, chronic bronchitis, hepatitis, pancreatitis, nephritis, trypsin deficiency, and idiopathic epilepsy. Acute trypsin deficiency can lead to pancreatic damage and then to death. Some FIH patients have developed severe personality changes, which were modified after removing the offending food allergen. Recheck the section on *Allergies* in Chapter III for the techniques of freeing a dog from allergies, especially those that are food-induced.

Good Protein Foods

Proteins in pet foods come primarily from meats, although excellent protein is available to your dog from dairy products (cottage cheese, farmer cheese, ricotta, cow's milk, goat's milk; and hard cheeses such as edam, gouda, swiss, münster, mild cheddar), soft-boiled eggs, wheat and rye berries and grasses, and sprouts such as alfalfa, lentils, and mung beans. Hypersensitivities aside, what is in the meats we feed our pets that is both good and bad? What shall we look for when seeking out that natural pet food?

Liver is one of the finest foods you can feed an animal, but in moderation. It is an extremely rich food with a very high phosphorus level, in relation to calcium, so you should be giving calcium supplementation along with it. It has a high vitamin and mineral content. However, the liver is a storehouse for many toxic wastes, so as far as possible try to find liver not heavily tainted with DES, tranquilizers, and antibiotics.

Poultry is a natural source of protein for the dog. It is high in the B-complex vitamins and minerals. Poultry fat is very high in linoleic acid and therefore helpful in maintaining good health in skin and coat. Chicken that has been frozen is quite indigestible to the pet as such; it needs a quick parboiling to ensure digestibility. Never give chicken, or other poultry bones to your dog, regardless of the size of bone or the size of dog. Poultry, when eaten in the wilds from a freshly killed carcass, is soft, tender, and digestible. Raw bones are clothed in hairy skin, guarding against puncture of the stomach wall or the intestine. But when cooked, to fit modern needs, the cooked chicken bones become brittle and can splinter, hurting the animal's intestinal tract.

When buying poultry meal or poultry by-products in your commercial pet food, try to find whether the product is from birds that were non-hormone-fed (that is, from organically raised chickens, also referred to as free-running or scratching chickens). Also be sure it contains no fecal matter or feathers as filler.

Fish is a good source of high-biological-value protein for dogs as well as cats. Since it contains high-biological-value protein, it is more completely usable to the animal. Fishmeal is very high in the essential amino acid taurine. Fish is a very good source of multiminerals, natural sea salts, unsaturated fatty acids (vitamin F), and, of course, essential amino acids. Mackerel and herring are rich in fats, vitamin B, and minerals; tuna fish and whitefish are also good. Fish should also be parboiled, like poultry, if it has been frozen, to remove the unnatural stiffening of the flesh. When buying commercial fish products, try to find out what kinds of fish are in the pet food; if it contains fecal waste, scales, heads, only racks, or also some flesh. Racks are the bones without any flesh. They are a fine source of multiminerals, but it would be preferable to have them balanced out with some kind of fish flesh as well.

Beef is, as mentioned before, a highly antigenic food, frequently tainted with DES (diethylstilbestrol), the synthetic female hormone, and a high-level residue of antibiotics and tranquillizing drugs. All meats, in certain circumstances, can cause the formation of excess uric acid. If an animal has difficulty with pancreatic function, beef would not be the meat of choice. More digestible meats would be poultry, lamb, and mutton. Beef is what most people think of when they look for meat for their pets. On balance, it is not the most preferable source of protein for your animal. Rather keep in mind the other meats, and fish, cottage cheese, eggs, and milk.

You have been given a crash course in many basic aspects of pet nutrition; all this in the hope that you will become a more educated consumer, better able to evaluate the relative merits and disadvantages of a variety of pet foods. Should you shop the supermarket shelves in utter frustration, finding little or nothing of what we discussed here, one course of action is to write to your favorite manufacturers. Encourage them to make meaningful changes in the right direction. These letters are vital to industry. Manufacturers do listen when the people speak. If they feel the pulse of public consciousness changing, then it becomes economically expedient for them to change in recognition of that pulse.

You can also use your ingenuity to make immediate changes in your older dog's diet. Remember, time is no longer on his side. Every nutritional innovation you make now will help to ensure that your beloved pet will live a longer, happier, healthier life. As you see the fruits of your inventive labor show in his glowing eyes, his gleaming fur, spritely step, and vivacious personality, you will experience a feeling of great joy, knowing your efforts have been for that most specially beloved of creatures: your older dog!

Dream takes Flirt and Fluffy for a walk.
A dog is neither too young nor too old
to be taught obedience.

Chapter VII

OBEDIENCE AND THE OLDER DOG

Introduction

In our earlier book, *How to Train Your Dog in Six Weeks*, we dealt with the puppy—his training, housebreaking, and problem solving—and on into the young-adult-dog phase, with a specialized, in-depth obedience course for him. By "in-depth" we refer to the classification of dog personalities by type, such as "high strung," "aggressive," or "overfriendly." Each of these personality types requires a special and somewhat different methodology to achieve the maximum response from the dog in training. The secret is to be able to correctly diagnose your dog's personality type, and then to tailor the obedience to complement his own personality quirks. This is preferable to bucking or denying characteristics, or exacerbating traits such as fear or aggression because of a simplistic, unilateral approach to obedience training.

A good professional dog trainer, because of the vast experience he has had with many different dogs, has the acuity to detect quickly and to interpret accurately each different personality nuance in a dog. A professional trainer possesses a special perception to be able to interact with a dog and outwit his elaborately amusing maneuvers, or to help to socialize and to adjust to normal a very reticient, fearful canine who has never been exposed to the world of people. To be able to reach the maximum degree of communication with them, one must be able to think as a dog, with the dog's rationalizations, the dog s irresistible desires, and the dog's conceptualizations of his most horrendous plight in life. The professional has a counter to each ploy or trick the dog attempts.

Dogs can read your strengths and weaknesses. They respect you for understanding them, and they also know when you've got their number. If you have control over a situation and take an implacable stand, insofar as your discipline requirements are concerned, your pet will read the signal loud and clear; in the long run he will be much happier for your wise administration of guidelines and boundaries. Sharing a common household is a most delightful experience when there is recognition of mutual responsibilities. Each of you gives of yourself to the other, developing the bond of interaction into a vital and enriching exchange. By following the advice in this book, you will be utilizing the dog-proven techniques used and developed by Bill Landesman, Director of Happy Tails Training Academy in New York's Nassau County. You will gain maximum communication between you and your dog and, having accomplished this, you will have effected a mutual respect, the dog for you and, certainly, you for what your pet has become.

In this book we cover the adult dog as he or she approaches middle age and advances on to the respected status of senior citizen. Beyond senior citizenship, we deal with the death of your beloved pet—its psychology as well as its other aspects. Then, as day follows night, we go back to the beginning again with a new puppy introduced into your household. Aware of your new addition, we provide a housebreaking and puppy-problem-solving routine to start the two of you off on a most harmonious track.

In this chapter we furnish a sane and rational obedience program for the older dog, should you have recently acquired one. Or perhaps you have led a hedonistic coexistence with your pet prior to this time. We have already taken into account the changes in personality of the aging dog, how he interacts with young children, and the consideration to be given by you and the children in accomodating.

It is important that your dog always think of you in the proper way. By that we mean your dog should view you in the proper perspective within the relationship you both share. This "proper" relationship is at its best when begun early in your dog's life. Many misguided people want their dogs to be "happy" and to be their friends; they don't want to exercise a master-slave relationship with the family pet. What they do not realize is that the permissiveness usually involved with letting a dog be "happy" creates a total lack of respect by that "happy" dog for his owner. It is also an incorrect assumption that a well-disciplined dog is unhappy. Knowing right from wrong, and having clearly defined boundaries, makes your dog much more confident and therefore a happier animal. A sensible obedience program, begun when he is young, will guarantee the establishment of the proper relationship between you and your dog. The younger the better, but, if you have an older dog, he still can be obedience-trained with excellent results. The fallacy that "you can't teach an old dog new tricks" is disproved almost daily by Bill Landesman and his staff of dog trainers, as they successfully train hundreds of dogs each year, many of which are more than five years old.

By faithfully following the simple obedience routine given here, you will be able to train any dog, young or old. This will assure adequate communication between you and your dog, and will also serve to educate him as to what is right and wrong for him. For a more comprehensive obedience routine, which deals with dogs by behavior type and personality, refer to our other book, *How to Train Your Dog in Six Weeks.* You will find it useful as a permanent-reference training guide. The text is profusely illustrated with clear, easy-to-follow pictures. The actual training of your dog, will cost you nothing but your time. Yet it will serve as the most wonderful present you could ever give to your dog, no matter what his age.

YOUR DOG MUST LEARN THE "RULES" BEFORE HE GETS OLD.

Obedience training can certainly be accomplished at any age, yet we must use discretion when training the older dog, since obedience training is psychologically demanding. We should differentiate between old and seriously infirm. To effect a good program of obedience, we must always have infinite patience. But, with the older dog, we sometimes need more patience and gentleness than usual. The older dog is approached with the same basic techniques as his more youthful counterpart, but certain compensations should be made. Hand signals need to be more distinct, to accommodate a gradual failing eyesight. Verbal commands should be extra clear and lengthened to counteract any possible hearing impairment. When in doubt, the learning or placing phase of obedience can and should always be carried on for an extra few days to an extra week. We don't want to encourage resistance by exerting weak corrections, so we must compensate with extra placement. A dog who is older will not move as quickly as he did in his prime. If your dog is not taking advantage of you but is simply sitting more slowly, then you must allow those extra few seconds before exerting a sit correction. Should the dog be arthritic or suffer from serious hip dysplasia, you may want to dispense with the SIT command altogether and just have your dog do a Stand-Stay at your side when you stop. In this way you will have heeling control without discomforting the dog unfairly. Once your older dog is sitting with reasonable speed and comfort, it takes very little extra effort to make him stay. A Sit-Stay increases your control over the sit.

A dog who finds it hard to negotiate walking, or one who lies down and gets up very slowly, will have to be placed on the down for an extra week, on a soft surface, so he won't resent it. In this training you will not be calling your dog to you from a Down-Stay (only from a Sit-Stay), so your Down-Stay will be more solid. When you return to heel your dog off, he may very well require more time to get up from the Down-Stay than from the Sit-Stay. This holds true even with a young healthy dog. So you must have extra patience allowing him to rise as you give the command to HEEL.

Dogs very often tell you when they are in pain, although not always. Should you find the down placement very painful for your dog, and should he find it painful to lie down apart from his obedience lesson, then it may be more judicious to dispense with the DOWN command altogether. These conditions vary with the individual dog, so that ultimately you have to trust in your own evaluation of the situation and then follow your inclinations. In no instance do we want

Obedience training can be accomplished regardless of a dog's size, breed, or age.

to obedience-train an older dog at the expense of his reasonably physical and mental comfort. The Down-Stay serves to keep the dog out of your hair, and your company's lap, for longer periods of time than a Sit-Stay. With an effective Down-Stay, you need not shoo him away in a strategic retreat to the basement or bathroom. Chances are that your older dog is fit enough to pester company. If this be so, then he is certainly fit enough to learn the down.

In obedience training you must behave like a cool, calm machine. You will be able to hold out longer, with less exhaustion, and your dog will learn more easily and more rapidly, realizing that you have the situation under control. Dogs will take advantage of their owners' weaknesses, even at an older age, and this will only mean more difficult, resentful training, with more discomfort for both of you. Speak and act calmly, slowly, deliberately, rationally, and consistently if you want to maximize your training potential and the subsequent benefits that accrue both to you and to your older dog.

The older dog is no longer as efficient at regulating his body temperature. Fats are responsible for this. The older dog often tends to lose weight and some of the fatty components of his body. In effect, he is not that well insulated anymore. So, when obedience-training the older dog, you must take care not to work him in extremes of heat and cold. This holds true for any dog, but more so for the older dog.

Constipation and incontinence can also be problems. It is important to allow the dog to relieve himself before and after an obedience session. If a dog suffers incontinence during the course of training, just ignore it and clean up later. Don't allow a small puddle of urine to interfere with your training session. It is also important not to feed your dog just prior to or after an obedience-training session. Feeding before can upset his digestion, and feeding after can not only cause indigestion but can be interpreted as a bribe. This we never want to do. Don't work your older dog to exhaustion. Several short sessions are always preferable to one long one.

Follow the training procedures as outlined in this chapter. If your dog seems to need any of the special modifications mentioned in this introduction, make them without hesitation. Obedience training will be rewarding no matter what the dog's age, and almost regardless of any handicap. Follow the same basic procedures with the handicapped dog. If you have a very special problem that has not been discussed in this book, either write to the authors or enlist the help and guidance of a professional trainer.

SIT-STAY OFF LEASH.

As Dream and Flirt exemplify, good obedience training is important at any age.

DOWN-STAY OFF LEASH.

Equipment

Any dog who is in good physical condition and has reached six months of age or older can begin the following training program. Proper equipment is very simple and easy to secure. You will need a strong metal chain collar, commonly and incorrectly referred to as a "choke" collar. This collar must be the correct size for your dog, and must be correctly installed on him if it is to work effectively. The correct size is two inches longer than his exact neck circumference. The collar must fit snugly, but not so tightly that it may injure his ears in the process of putting it on or taking it off. The collar must not be so big that it can slip off or get snagged on branches or furniture when he walks around. For proper collar installation, see the accompanying photo.

Next you will need a good strong leash that must be six feet in length. Anything longer or shorter would be useless for obedience-training a dog. This six-foot leash should have a loop at one end and a bolt snap at the other end. The leash should be made of leather or a web-canvas material. Chain-link leashes must not be used as they would cause the handler or trainer more discomfort than his dog.

The Attention-Getter

Find yourself a suitable training area, such as a backyard or even the front of your house at a quiet time of day. With your dog properly hooked up to collar and leash, enter the training area and begin to walk across it until you get to one end. Now just stop. Don't talk to your dog. Don't praise him; just completely ignore him. Pick a spot on the other side of your area and, after about one minute, begin to walk to this spot. Your right-hand thumb should be through the end loop of the leash, with your hand closed on it. Your left hand should be clasped over your right. Allow the entire six feet of leash between you and your dog. As you walk across your training area, your dog may be reacting in a number of possible ways. He could be indulging in a variety of antics from walking or running near you to lying down and refusing to walk.

Whatever his reaction to your silent routine of walking, stopping, and walking, you must continue this routine, undeterred by his antics. Continue walking from point to point across the area, stopping, and ignoring your dog when you reach each point. After resting for about one minute you will head for the other point, where you will again rest a minute, and then walk back to the first point. Do not coax your dog if he is unwilling to walk. Just continue walking yourself, and

The proper equipment: A six-foot web leash and a metal chain collar.

Use a two-inch running lead for proper collar fit.

The incorrect way to install a chain collar. The collar will not release.

The correct way to install a chain collar. Form the letter "P."

drag him along with you. He will soon be walking. Your dog must learn that you do not need his permission to walk and that when he is attached to you by a leash he must walk when you do. The title of this section is "The Attention-Getter," which means that before we teach your dog to sit or heel or do anything else, we are first going to get his attention firmly focused on you, the handler. In other words, what we are going to teach your dog is that he should WATCH YOU! As you silently walk across your training area, your dog may lunge wildly away from you, trying to pull the leash out of your hands. If he lunges, just get a good grip on the end of your leash and continue your routine. Work your dog for two fifteen-minute sessions, each followed by a five-minute break on the leash (with you holding the end). After the second break, end the lesson by telling him OKAY in a bright, cheerful voice, and leave the area. Your dog should be left alone for about a half hour after the training session, to think it over. He should never get sympathy or lavish praise and coddling from you or anyone else after a lesson. This would convince him that what you did in obedience training was wrong or unfair to him, and it would prevent him from developing the proper attitude toward his training sessions.

The incentive for your dog to watch you is provided by your silent handling. The less you communicate, the more he will watch you, and this is the most important lesson you can ever teach your dog. Your dog should be worked for four days on the same silent routine, walking back and forth between the two predetermined spots. By the fourth day you will be pleasantly surprised to see your dog walking when you begin to walk, stopping fairly close to you when you stop, and reacting in a very calm, relaxed way when you work him. And as you walk you will be most pleased to see him frequently turning his head to watch you. In four days you have taught him to *watch you*, and all *without* saying a word to him!

On the fifth day the training routine will change. You will introduce a distraction at one end of your training area. The distraction should not appear until you have been working your dog for at least a few minutes. The distraction can be someone holding a cat, clanging two pots together, waving his arms around, etc. Anything is fair, so long as the distraction is confined to one side of your training area. You have entered the area with your dog on the six-foot training leash. You should be holding the end loop with both hands. The distraction should appear suddenly, such as a person holding a cat stepping out from the corner of a building. As your dog lunges toward the

The Attention-Getter.

distraction, you should execute a quick right-about turn and run in the opposite direction. When your dog runs out of leash, the impact should jerk him back toward you. This jerk must be administered by you *silently*! After the correction, your dog may stand watching you with a puzzled look on his face. Most likely, one correction won't suffice. He may just get up, shrug it off, and make another charge toward the distraction. This is fine. Your reaction will not be to hold him back. On the contrary, you will invite him to lunge by moving again toward the distraction. When he does, you will again make a right-about turn and run forcefully in the opposite direction. Whether it takes one, two, or twenty corrections, your dog will finally stand in close proximity to you, with his eyes focused on you and not on the distraction.

Start walking back and forth again within your training area, working your dog with the appropriate stops at each end. Be certain not to move any closer than fifteen feet from the distraction. Any renewed charges by your dog will be handled with the same right-about turn and accompanying silent correction on your part. At the end of each fifteen-minute session, give your dog a five-minute break on the leash. This does not mean that he should run around the yard like an uncontrollable maniac, dragging the leash on his break. Take the break with him, at one of your stopping points, by just sitting down near him. After two fifteen-minute sessions, followed by the two five-minute breaks, remove the distraction from your training area, and leave the area with your dog. Give your dog a half-hour alone after the lesson, to think over the training session that has just ended.

Work your dog with a distraction, as you have done on this fifth day, for two more additional days. His attention and respect for you should be growing. After the seventh day you should have your dog's complete attention. You are now ready to begin heeling.

Heeling

Heeling means that your dog will walk by your left side without pulling, walking when you walk, and stopping when you stop. When starting out on the heeling command, it is important for you to begin heeling on your *left foot*. It was important too with the young dog, but not as important as with the older dog. He is ready at your left side and your left foot is closest to him. Since his eyesight is not as good as it used to be, we are giving him an extra advantage or benefit by clearly stepping out on the left foot, so that, whatever his sharpness of vision, he can better understand and react to the command of HEEL.

Proper heeling—front view.

Proper heeling—side view.

On the first day of heeling, enter the training area with your dog on the usual six-foot training leash. There should be no distractions present today.

There is a special way to hold the leash, doubled up and secured with both hands. Study the accompanying photos. Proper leash grip is vitally important to the success of this training and no deviation from it is possible. To properly take up the leash, place your right-hand thumb through the end loop of the leash. Now grab the leash about fifteen inches from its beginning, at the dog's end, and put this portion over your right thumb again. Now, with your left hand, grab everything directly below your right hand. Your hands should be together and touching as if you were holding a baseball bat.

To begin heeling, just command, Dream, HEEL. First you speak the dog's name, Dream, and then follows the command word HEEL. Dream, HEEL is more of a warning than a command to your dog. It is warning him that you are about to move. He is not supposed to do anything when you say Dream, HEEL. You are supposed to begin walking. So now as you tell him, Dream, HEEL, begin to walk across your training area. If your dog refuses to walk or holds back, trying to stop you, your response should not be to coax but, conversely, you should break out into a fast run. Speed up into this run for ten or fifteen feet and, as he comes up alongside, slow down to a normal walking pace. The dog that uses the tactic of holding back is trying to end the lesson. He would rather go to sleep or play somewhere. Your dog realizes that to train him you need to walk with him. He thinks that if he can stop your movements or maneuvers, then he can end the lesson. This is correct—he can. You, however, must be the one who wins out, no matter how much he holds back. You must run until he sees that it is easier for him to walk with you than to resist. Nothing your dog does must stop you from walking.

Whether or not you have to run with him, once he is walking with you he will sooner or later get too far in front of you and begin to pull. When this happens, you should correct him by making a silent and very abrupt right-about turn, quickly walking in the opposite direction. Each time he gets out in front of you, you should make your silent right-about turn. Your dog has the surprising discomfort of being caught unawares by your quick turns, and he soon will begin to hang back, watching you, in order to avoid the turns and their accompanying unpleasant corrections. This is the beginning of heeling. After a few right-about turns, as your dog hangs back and begins to walk calmly at your side, come to a stop and, as he stops at your side,

100

Taking up the leash, place loop over right thumb.

Place middle section of leash over right thumb again.

Final correct leash grip.

101

Right about turn.

praise him. No, don't bribe him with cookies. Just praise him, show-ing him you are pleased with him, by patting his head and telling him, GOOD BOY, VERY GOOD. Then give a new HEEL com-mand, Dream, HEEL, and move off, walking across your area. Each time he gets out in front, you should correct with a turn, and each time he hangs back you should bring him up to your side, not by jerking on the leash but by running. You should not talk to him at all, except to tell him, Dream, HEEL, as you begin to walk. We repeat once again, the *right-about turns are to be made silently.* You should also praise him each time you both stop.

Work your dog for fifteen minutes, followed by a five-minute break. Then work him for a second fifteen minutes, followed by another five-minute break. Let that end the day's training session. Remember that the five-minute breaks are taken with the dog. Leave your dog alone for at least one-half hour after the lesson, to think over what has happened. Never romp and play with your dog right after a training session; it would undo all you have accomplished. Re-peat this heeling routine in training sessions for three more days. After this time your dog should be walking at your side without pul-ling you.

On the fifth day of heeling you should again have a distraction at one end of your training area. Enter the area with your dog and heel him toward the distraction. When he charges toward it, make a quick, hard right-about turn and walk swiftly in the opposite direction, away from the distraction. Then make another right-about turn and again head down toward the distraction. If your dog hangs back and walks by your side, stop and praise him. If he runs out in front of you again, again make a hard right-about turn, walking away from the distraction. This should again be followed by another right-about turn, walking back toward the distraction. You should work your dog in this way—toward, then away from the distraction—until he walks toward the distraction at your side, without pulling, and stops for praise each time you stop. Most dogs trained by our school, Happy Tails, stop pulling after three or four of these silent turnabout corrections. The rest of them gave up after fewer than ten corrections.

Work your dog for the usual two fifteen-minute sessions, followed by two five-minute breaks. For the next two days, repeat the work of this fifth day's training routine, with a distraction at one end.

The Sit

On this first day of the sit, there should be no distractions in the training area. Begin by working your dog on the heeling routine, with the appropriate right-about turns if his pulling makes them necessary. Once he is warmed up and working well, come to a stop. This stop will be different from all previous ones because you will not praise him for stopping at your side. Instead, you will place him on a sit, in the following way. As you stop, tighten up on the leash with your right hand, directly over your dog's head, and exert a steady upward pressure on his neck with the leash. At the same time, your left hand should push his rear end down toward the ground until he is forced

The SIT placement.

to sit. As you push or place him into the sitting position, you will command, Dream, SIT. You will not repeat the command. You will only give *one* command, immediately placing him on the sit. As soon as he is sitting, you will praise him and then walk off as you command him, Dream, HEEL. After a few more moments of walking, again come to a stop. Command, Dream, SIT, and immediately place him on the sit. Continue working on heeling and the sit for this day's two fifteen-minute work sessions, followed by the usual two breaks.

On the second day of the sit you should continue placing your dog on sits exactly as you did yesterday. Today's routine will vary in that you will begin making left and right turns, as well as the previous right-about turns that you used in your heeling routine. Left turns are *not* left-about turns, but are ninety-degree turns made into the dog. This turn corrects a dog, not for lunging in front of you, but for just leading slightly in front of you, maybe six or twelve inches. A quick, abrupt left turn made directly into the dog will keep him watching you closely and thus improve his alignment in heel position. Remember to say nothing as you make the left turn. It must come as a complete surprise in order to be effective. The left turn can be made more effective by bringing your knees up into the dog as you collide with him during your turns. The more unpleasant you make it, the more attentive he will be to avoid getting caught by your left turn, and that means he will have to hang back and watch you. This is precisely the result that we want.

Right turns will correct the dog who is heeling widely—in other words, too far away from you, his handler. Be aware, this is not a right-about turn but a ninety-degree turn to your right. Your dog will receive a jolt on the leash as you make the right turn. This surprise can be made more effective by a quicker and wider first step as you are making the turn. Your dog will soon realize that his wide heeling is causing the unpleasant right turns and that the turns do not occur when he walks close to you. Your consistency will make his choice clear. See the accompanying diagram for the proper technique in making each turn. Work your dog as directed above for the usual two fifteen-minute sessions, each followed by a five-minute break. For the following three days, work your dog exactly as you have done on this second day's teaching of the sit. No distractions need be present.

On the sixth day your routine should change again. Enter your training area with your dog at heel position and begin working him on a few turns for about one minute. Then shorten up on the leash and come to a stop. As you stop, command, Dream, SIT. If your dog

SILENT HEELING TURNS

1. RIGHT ABOUT TURN

CORRECTS DOG THAT IS LUNGING
OR PULLING OUT IN FRONT OF YOU.

2. LEFT TURN

CORRECTS DOG THAT IS LEADING
SLIGHTLY IN FRONT OF YOU. THIS
TURN IS MADE DIRECTLY INTO DOG.

3. RIGHT TURN

CORRECTS DOG THAT IS
HEELING WIDE (TOO FAR
FROM YOU.)

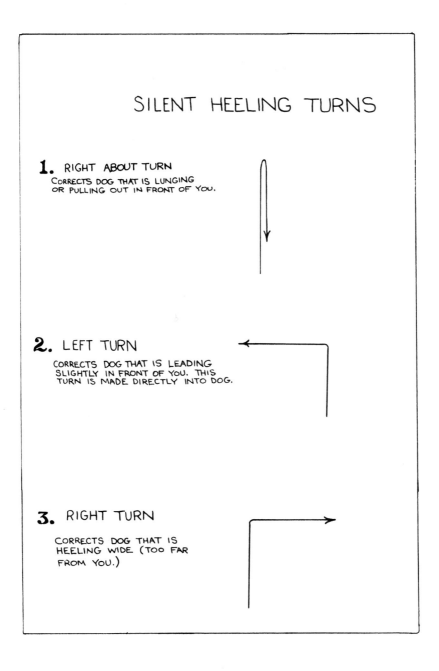

sits, praise him. If not, jerk forcefully on the leash, with both hands, in an upward direction. Your correction should be so hard that it forces your dog to sit. If he sits, praise him. If your dog is still not sitting, you probably haven't corrected hard enough. So now, repeat the command, Dream, SIT, and this time correct properly—that is, very hard. When your dog sits, praise him. Then move off with a new HEEL command, Dream, HEEL. After a few more turns, again come to a stop. As you do, command, Dream, SIT. If your dog sits, praise him and heel him off. If he does not sit, correct as before, very hard. When he sits, praise him and move off with a new HEEL command. Continue working your dog in this way, correcting forcefully when necessary. Work your dog on the above routine for the usual two fifteen-minute sessions, each followed by a five-minute break. For the seventh day, repeat the sixth day's procedure.

On the eighth day you should work your dog exactly as before, except that the initial sit command should be omitted when you come to a stop. You should stop silently, and if your dog does not sit you should correct forcefully. We will now require an automatic sit from your dog each time you stop, without a command from you. This forces your dog to watch you closely and, once again, this is our main objective. Give him two fifteen-minute sessions and the usual breaks on this eighth day of the sit.

On the ninth day repeat the previous day's procedure, using a distraction at one end of your training area. Work toward the distraction and away from it, toward it and away, frequently stopping, and remembering to enforce the automatic sit when you must.

The Sit-Stay

On the first day of the Sit-Stay, enter the area with no distractions present. Begin working your dog on heeling turns and automatic sits. When he is warmed up and working well, come to a stop. After he sits, let go of the leash with your left hand, and push your open left hand toward his face. Your palm should be toward his nose, as you command. Dream, STAY. Step out, beginning with your right foot, and turn to face him, exerting a slight upward pressure on the leash, with your right hand. Keep your extended left hand in front of his face. After five seconds, step back to his side, release the tension on the leash, and praise him. Then move off with a new HEEL command, Dream, HEEL. Continue working your dog on about-turns, right-angle turns, left turns, and sits. After a couple of minutes, come to a stop. When your dog sits, again command, Dream,

106

The SIT correction.

The STAY hand signal.

STAY. Step out and turn facing him, maintaining upward tension on the leash with your right hand, while your open left hand remains in his face. After five seconds, step back to his side, praise him, and move off, together with a new HEEL command. Continue working your dog in this manner that day and for the next two days.

On the fourth day of the stay your routine will differ only in that, when you command, Dream, STAY, you will drop your left hand by your side after giving your dog the proper STAY signal. Release the tension on the leash with your right hand, and step back one step. After ten seconds, return to his side, take up the leash, and praise him. Then move off with a new HEEL command. Work the stay, the automatic sit, and the various turns for the first fifteen-minute session. Then give your dog a five-minute break.

After the break, when you again work your dog on the entire routine, the stay will progress even further. When you stop and he sits, swing your open left hand toward his face and command, Dream, STAY. Leave on your right foot, and step back the entire six-foot length of the leash. There is no tension in the leash at this time. After ten seconds return to his side, take up the leash (as he waits), praise him, and then heel him off. Continue the entire routine, with all the Sit-Stays at the full six-foot length of the leash away from the dog. After the usual fifteen-minute session, give him a

The SIT-STAY from six feet away.

break and end the lesson for the day. It will be helpful to your dog if you take off on your right foot when you leave him on a stay. It will help him further if you take off on your left foot, because it's nearest to him, when you give your dog the HEEL command. At this stage of the Sit-Stay, you are returning to your dog's side before he really has a chance to break the stay, thus gradually building him up.

Work your dog just as above on the next day's sessions, with ten-second Sit-Stays at six feet. On the sixth day you should vary the Sit-Stay part of your training routine, in that, after leaving your dog on the stay, you should walk forward the six feet, turn and face him, and not return until twenty seconds have elapsed. We will now begin to correct your dog if he breaks the Sit-Stay. When you have left him on a Sit-Stay, your dog is allowed to look around. But, if he attempts to stand up, as his rear end comes up off the ground you should jerk sharply on the leash and, after a slight pause, command, Dream, SIT, Dream, STAY. You should not return close to your dog to correct him. You must prove to him that you can correct at a distance if you want him to work at a distance. If your dog moves toward you as you correct, step back away from him and maintain the six-foot distance between you. The jerk of your correction should catch your dog *as* he stands up, and before he can even take a step. This correction must not be a powerful tug that pulls the dog toward you. Instead, it must be a lightning-fast, sharp jerk of the leash, only hard enough to knock him back down. If, after the correction, he remains standing, command, Dream, SIT. If he still remains standing, correct again (from six feet away). Then command, Dream, SIT. You should alternate command and correction in this way until you win out and he is sitting, no matter how long it takes. Once your dog has sat, you should hold up your hand, from six feet away, and repeat, Dream, STAY. Anytime your dog breaks a Sit-Stay, you should correct in this way, alternating commands and corrections, until he is sitting once again. You can then return, take up the leash, and praise him. Work your dog on the entire routine of heeling, turns, automatic sits, and Sit-Stays, correcting when needed. Work him for the usual two fifteen-minute sessions, followed by the two regular five-minute breaks.

The seventh day's work will vary in that you should begin to return to your dog, when he is on a stay, going around counterclockwise behind him, and then back to heel position. (See the diagrams on the next page for the proper return.) To return properly, switch the leash to your left hand, and walk slowly toward your dog. The

THE ARROW SHOWS THE PROPER COUNTER-CLOCKWISE RETURN TO YOUR DOG FROM A STAY.

CENTER OF LEASH RESTS ON FLOOR.

HOLD YOUR LEFT FIST TOWARD HIS FACE AS YOU RETURN...

LEASH REMAINS TOUCHING FLOOR AS YOU CONTINUE MOVING AROUND DOG.

REMEMBER TO TAKE UP THE LEASH BEFORE PRAISING YOUR DOG.

center of the leash should just touch the floor. Your left fist should be held about one foot in front of the dog's face as you walk around, counterclockwise, behind him, and stop at his side in the heel position. You should then take up the leash, praise him, and move on with a new HEEL command. Your dog should be able to hold for almost a minute on his Sit-Stay today. Building him up gradually is the best way. From now on, you should always return around *behind* your dog, unless told otherwise.

The eighth day's work should be with a distraction present in your training area. Work twenty- to forty-second Sit-Stays, correcting when you must. Work on the entire routine with appropriate corrections where needed, and remember always, from now on, to return counterclockwise around and behind your dog.

The Down

The DOWN command should mean to you and your dog that you want him to lie down prone on the ground. This is the hardest command of all to teach any dog. The reason is that, to your dog, the DOWN is not just another command; although, to us, it is merely another very practical command among many. Practical because in a Down-Stay position he can *stay* much longer than he can on a Sit-Stay. He can also resist greater distractions in the down that he can while on a sit. But, unfortunately, in a dog's mind, when you tell him to lie down you are not just making another command. In his mind you are asking him to submit to you completely, physically and psychologically. This is significant, in that such behavior is handed down to dogs by their ancestors, the wolves, who submit to each other in this way. Every fiber in a dog's body tells him not to lie down for you, and most dogs will resist the down command much more than any other. To make this command as easy as possible for your dog to learn, proceed as follows.

On the first day of the down, enter your training area and work your dog on his entire routine. There should be no distractions present. As soon as he is warmed up and working well, come to a stop. When he sits, command, Dream, STAY, but do not leave. Instead, place your dog Down in the following manner. Drop the leash by your feet close enough to step on or grab if needed. Place your left hand on his back and bend low, so that with your right hand you can reach around, palm up, knuckles down, under his right front leg and grab his left one. Command, Dream, DOWN, and with one smooth motion, pull slightly up and forward with your right arm, while you

111

The DOWN placement.

press firmly down on his back with your left hand or forearm. You should place your dog down smoothly, giving only one command as you do so. Usually, after being placed down, the dog's front paws will be fouling the leash. By that we mean the leash may be tangled around his paws, preventing you from gathering up the leash smoothly and moving on. It is important that your dog does *not* learn that he can bring a halt to the lesson by fouling the leash in this way. To prevent that from happening, grab the leash close to his neck, with your right hand, after he is down, and command, Dream, HEEL, as you walk away. You will then be able to take up the leash properly, and your dog will be unaware of any lost chance to halt the lesson.

Continue working your dog, placing him down in the manner described, alternating with Sit-Stays and just automatic sits, for the remainder of the day's two work sessions. For the next four days you should continue placing your dog down and continue working on the rest of the routine, gradually increasing the length of time on the Sit-Stays to one full minute.

On the sixth day of the down the routine will change drastically. We have spent the past five days teaching your dog what the command DOWN means. We can now be certain that he knows and we can begin to correct him if he refuses to lie down on command. Work

112

your dog on his entire routine. When he is warmed up and working well, come to a stop and tell him to STAY, but don't leave. Instead, turn and face him. You should be close to him, only one foot away and directly in front of him. Command, Dream, DOWN. The leash is slack in your hands. If your dog lies down, return to the heel position by his side and praise him. If he does not lie down after four seconds, correct him as follows. With both hands together on the leash, move your hands slowly to about five inches from his face, creating even more slack. Then, with a sudden forceful jerk in a *downward* direction, and slightly to your left, correct very hard and silently. Your correction should actually knock your dog off his feet, into the down position. Once he is down, return to heel by his side, praise him, and move off with a new HEEL command. If your first correction does not cause your dog to lie down, you have most likely not corrected hard enough. Be sure not to repeat this mistake. Command a second time, Dream, DOWN. Then, after four seconds, correct your dog with sufficient force to knock him down. Move to the heel position, praise him, and walk on with a new HEEL command. On this occasion you should return right to your dog's side, once he is down; do not walk counterclockwise around and behind him as you have recently been doing on the Sit-Stay.

After working on a Sit-Stay and some heeling turns, again come to a stop. Tell your dog to STAY. Turn and face him and, with both hands on the leash, command, Dream, DOWN. If he lies down, praise him. If not, correct (very hard) as before. (Remember, all cor-

The DOWN correction.

113

rections for the down are in a downward direction, as opposed to sit corrections, which are in an upward direction.) As soon as he is down, return to heel position, praise him, and move off with a new HEEL command. Continue working on the down, correcting when you must, until your dog performs six downs in a row with no corrections being necessary. You must not stop after fifteen minutes today, but, instead, continue working him until your dog gives you the required six downs in a row. Whether it takes three minutes or three hours, you should continue until you have the six downs. Then give your dog the usual five-minute break and, following the break, return to work, alternating the previous routines with the new down routine. By the end of this session your dog should be going down as you command, Dream, DOWN.

The seventh day we will turn our down into the useful Down-Stay. Come to a halt and, when your dog sits, from the heel position (do not turn and face him), command, Dream, DOWN. When he lies down, swing your open left hand back towards his face and command Dream, STAY. Leave and turn to face him from the six-foot length of the leash. Make the stays short in duration on the first day; you will gradually build them up. Return right to his side, today only, for the Down-Stays.

On the eighth day you can expect almost a full minute on the Down-Stay, and you can begin returning counterclockwise around behind your dog, as you have been doing on your returns from the Sit-Stay. You should have a distraction present in your training area today, and should correct hard, when it is needed, convincing your dog that watching you is a better thing for him to do than watching the distraction.

The Recall

People wonder why their dogs will not come when they call them. Lots of dogs add insult to injury not only by refusing to come, but by actually running away from their owners when they are called. The reasons why dogs refuse to come to their owners are many. They range from enjoying being chased (you after them when you call them), to remembering how you called them as puppies and then, when they did come, reprimanded them for some chewing or housebreaking transgression. If you have made running from you fun or coming to you a punishment, then we have to undo the negative training you have already unconsciously given your dog. To teach your dog to come when you call him, proceed as follows.

The DOWN-STAY from six feet away.

115

On the first day of the recall, begin working your dog on the entire obedience routine. When he is warmed up and working well, come to a stop and leave him on a Sit-Stay. As you face him from the six-foot distance of the leash, you should prepare to call him by switching the leash from your right to your left hand. Command, Dream, COME, and gesture in toward yourself with your right hand. Reel him in with the leash and, holding him directly in front of you, command, SIT. We not only require your dog to come, but then we require him to sit directly in front of and facing you. It is important to note at this time that you must make an exception if your dog does not sit after he has come directly in front of you. You should not correct him if he does not sit after coming. This would be similar to calling him, and punishing him after he has come. Only good things must follow his coming to you. If he comes to you and receives a correction, he will come no more. If your dog sits in front of you, praise him. If not, push his rear down, placing him on a sit, and praise him.

Your recall is not over yet. Your dog must now *finish*. This means that on an additional HEEL command from you, he will walk clockwise around and behind you, stopping by your left side at heel position, and then sitting. To teach him this, you should start by walking him through the finish in the following way: after your dog is sitting in front of you, you holding the entire leash in your right hand only, place your right hand behind you against your back. The leash should be taut, so that any further backward movement of your body would drag your dog toward you. Now command, Dream, HEEL, and take a full step to the rear with your right foot. As you take this first rearward step, your dog will be pulled along at your right side as he begins to respond normally to your HEEL command. Your dog does not realize at this time that you are walking backwards. To him, he is just heeling to your left side, as usual. You should immediately take a second rearward step, this time with your left foot and, as you do so, change the leash, behind your back, from your right hand to your left hand alone. All rearward movement now halts. You then take a step forward with your left foot and this causes the dog to pass around behind you and wind up on your left side. As you come to a stop, holding the leash now with both hands, command, Dream, SIT. When he sits, praise him, and move off with a new HEEL command.

There is a danger concerning the recall that should be understood at this time. The recall actually is teaching your dog to *break* the Sit-Stay. Of course, it is only in a certain circumstance that this occurs (specifically, when you call him). But if too many recalls were

The RECALL.

Sitting in front of you after the
RECALL.

The FINISH.

Around to HEEL position.

done in sequence, the results could be that the Sit-Stay would be severely weakened and this could eventually destroy all of the obedience. Previously, your dog learned *never* to break a stay and that you would always return to him. Now, occasionally, you will begin calling him to you to end some Sit-Stays. This is all right, and no harm will result, so long as you mix up and vary the routine. Never do recalls again and again in repetition, but always vary the routine, alternating returns to his side with recalls. Give him long Sit-Stays, ending with you returning to him and praising him. This shows him that you still expect reliable stays.

Work recalls when your dog is on a Sit-Stay, but *not* when he is doing a Down-Stay. If your dog knows that you might call him on a sit, but have never called him while on a Down-Stay, then this will reserve the Down-Stay as a supersolid position for him. In case of emergency this will hold him longer and strengthen his Down-Stay, which could someday save his life.

After three more days you can start the next command, the Stand For Examination. As you begin the stand, your recall will improve until your dog comes, sits, and finishes all under his own power. Remember, eventually he must finish around you, with you not moving at all. This usually evolves through repetition in about two weeks time.

The Stand For Examination

The stand, is a practical, useful command for all dogs. It helps when you brush and groom them. It can also make a shy-afraid dog more confident as he learns to stand alone while being touched by a stranger. You cannot correct your dog for not standing or for breaking a stand. Instead, you must gradually build him up to the point where his confidence enables him to stand and stay.

The first day, begin by including your placing him up on stands in his regular work routine. Come to a stop, and when your dog sits by your side, pull steadily forward, not upward, on the leash with your right hand, while you bend forward and reach across and under your dog with your left hand, lifting up his stomach. As you do this, command, Dream, STAND. As he stands up, softly stroke his left side and calmly praise him, whispering, VERY GOOD, THAT'S MY BOY. After a few seconds, heel him forward one step, stop, and, when he sits at your side, praise him for the stand.

Continue this placing him on the stands for the next three days. The fourth day's work on the stand will differ, in that, once your dog

Placing on the STAND.

is standing, you should give him a soft STAY command and hand signal and move about two feet from his side. Then you should return directly to his side and take up the leash. Heel him forward one step, and praise him when he has sat.

On the fifth day you should STAND him, tell him to STAY, and move away the entire six-foot length of the leash. If at any time he sits down, you should just lift him up and repeat the commands, Dream, STAND, STAY.

The sixth day's work should be an exact repetition of the fifth. Your dog *never* is required to stand up under his own power. You should always place him or lift him to the stand position.

On the seventh day you should vary the routine of the stand by returning in the formal counterclockwise manner to your dog's side. As you walk around him to return, you should lightly touch his sides, rear, and even lightly begin to pull or shake his tail. The next two days should be an exact repetition of the seventh day's work.

On the tenth day you should STAND your dog, give a STAY command, and leave him, While you stand the six-foot length of the leash away, you should have a helper approach the dog from your right rear side. Your assistant should walk up to the dog, touching him lightly on the head, back, and rear. Then he should cross behind the dog and back behind you. Afterward, you should return counterclockwise around to your dog's side. You should not stroke your dog's sides. Only your assistant touches the dog at this final stage. Then heel him forward one step and, when he sits, praise him.

The next two weeks should include work on your entire obedience routine, with many varied distractions present in your training area. You should also work your dog among strange distractions and in unfamiliar places, such as busy shopping centers. When you have thoroughly built him up in all sorts of situations, you then have an interesting option available to you.

With your dog working well in distractions, you may wish to test yourself and your dog against the owners and their trained dogs. In newspapers or magazines you can locate Dog Shows that will include "Obedience Competition" matches. Your dog will only qualify at this stage of his training to enter the class called *SUB NOVICE* in obedience competition. You should feel quite confident in entering him and, if you do, you will most likely be happily surprised in that your dog will do very well. The reason for this is that the other dogs, and their owners, who will be competing against you will have been trained in group classes. Usually these classes are run by breeders or obedience judges who are *not* professional dog trainers. What they teach is a nagging, repetitive method of obedience rather than the positive "praise-correction" method we have used to train your dog. You will find that the superiority of your method of training will make you more than their equal, even though they may have been going to group classes for years and you have only been training your dog for a number of weeks.

Whether or not you choose to compete in dog shows, you have begun a relationship with your dog that, unfortunately, far too few dog owners ever even approach. Congratulations and, most importantly, keep working him!

Chapter VIII

COPING WITH DEATH

Our objective in this book has been to explore the mutual bond between you and your pet, and to do and suggest anything possible to nurture this harmonious alliance. The book is about life, but we must also face up to the finite certainty of death. And death is not a dirty word; it should not be viewed as the most horrible fate that can befall your dog. It is merely a part of the changing of life's seasons. A crucial element in the psychology of life versus death is acceptance. It is permissable to age. It is inevitable and acceptable to become infirm as age advances. But that should in no way alter the commitment between you and your pet.

We should also realize the unassailable truth that animals do not have the cerebral sophistication to comprehend the inevitability of death. They do not advance into senior citizen status with an abhorrence of their increasing age. Time is amorphous to animals. It does not hang heavy on their consciousness, as with many humans. So they do not value longevity as much as they esteem the timeliness of *here and now*. A pet is not only a pet, but assuredly one of the most enriching and rewarding interpersonal experiences that life has to offer to a human being.

Many people are not familiar with the varying life expectancies among dog breeds. Longevity normally ranges from eight to sixteen years. Many of us also may not realize that the largest breeds, the St. Bernard, Great Dane, and the Irish Wolfhound, can look forward to a life span only half that of the very small dogs such as the Toy Poodle, the Mini Schnauzer, or the Fox Terrier. But within the bounds of this data there exists a message of overriding importance: the quality of life is infinitely more important than its length.

In summary: Value the quality of your life together with your pet and, when his life span is ended, hold a special place in your memory for that very unique relationship. But do not become inactivated by grief. Celebrate the continuum of life through sharing, the sharing of your infinite love with a new puppy who vitally needs the affection that you alone have to give!

Practical Aspects of Dealing with Death

There are certain things concerning death with which every owner should be aquainted. Many practical considerations must be evaluated and alternatives discussed with your mate, simply as part of owning a dog. Death should not be scratching at your door before you begin to ponder reasonable alternatives in dealing with the eventuality of your dog's death. If you waited till the last minute to discuss your own respective deaths with your spouse or other loved ones, you would surely find yourselves eventually in a crisis situation where time could no longer accommodate soulful ruminations on alternatives. In human terms, the deceased would have abdicated their right to a choice in the personal matter of their own deaths. Though we do not and cannot ask a dog his preferences in these matters, we should—we must—ask ourselves and our family what collective decisions are to be implemented relevent to the death of the family pet.

Death is not to be feared nor to be looked upon as repulsive. Dogs that die simply go to sleep permanently. They look, to the average person, as if they are simply asleep. Death does not turn your dog into a hideous caricature. Your beautiful dog does not begin to decompose before your eyes, nor does he immediately discharge a repulsive odor. So you should have no fear in sharing this experience with the children if your dog dies in the house. Many older dogs die in their sleep, at night, when the body is at its lowest ebb. In such cases, you may just wake up in the morning and find him peacefully alseep without heartbeat or movement in his chest. His eyes may be closed or they may be open. If they are open, you will observe a glassiness or glaze to the eyeball. You will be able to tap the surface of the eye gently without receiving any response. That is one very accurate way of telling if death has come. Should you elicit no response, no blinking, no movement in the eyeball, then, for his sense of dignity, close the eyes. You can lift up his jowls and examine the gums. If they are white and lifeless, the blood has ceased pumping vital oxygen throughout his body. You can also examine the chest for movement and for heartbeat. When a dog is asleep, you can always notice some lung expansion as he inhales and exhales rhythmically. When he has ceased to breathe, there will be no heartbeat and no chest expansion. Certain muscles may twitch slightly, even after death, but this is only the remnants of electrical energy reacting in his muscles and nerve complexes and, unfortunately not a sign that he is still alive. It may seem to you slightly indelicate in your extremely distraught state, to be required to check your dog's vital life signs, such as the eyes, gums, chest, and heartbeat. But, if you do this and find that your dog is still alive, you will be saving precious time. Upon contacting your vet immediately, you will also make it easier for him to tell you what to do. You may have a chance to save the dog's life.

When animals (or humans) die, they lose control of their excretory functions. This is another sign of death, although animals under anesthesia can also display loss of control of excretory functions. Should you come upon your dog in the morning and, having established that he is dead, notice that he has urinated and defecated involuntarily during the night, don't be shocked. Clean it up as best you can and place him on a clean surface: a blanket preferably, which you can also cover him with. You are not going to keep the dog warm with the blanket, for his thermal sensitivity has left him. Yet there must be a dignity in death as well as in life. If your dog is nearing the end and he is home with you, put him on a blanket. If it becomes soiled, simply change blankets. You can use the blanket to carry him to the vet when the end does arrive.

If the family, or any special members of the family, feel the inclination to sit up the night with a dying dog, by all means do so. That is, do so if you are not so visibly shaken emotionally that you disturb your dog's final hours of life. If the dog is not in severe pain and is simply dying of old age, then there is no reason why his place should not be home with the family he has loved and who will always love him. Your dog should be celebrated in all phases of his existence, in death as well as in life. Sharing among the family an experience so natural, significant, and fundamental as the death of an older dog can serve to bring the family closer together. Sharing the death of a family pet can also serve to make the children less fearful of and more comfortable with death. When at all possible, a dog should remain at home for the end. This is much more comforting in his final moments than being transported to the antiseptic ambiance of a strange and busy veterinary hospital.

Euthanasia

On the matter of euthanasia, no one can tell you when to put your animal out of his suffering. You must be guided by what your vet tells you, what your pet conveys to you through his very distinct and meaningful language, and what your heart tells you. If you are at all in doubt as to the prognosis that your vet gives on the health status of your dog, get another professional opinion. When in doubt, don't ever proceed hastily with euthanasia. After the loss of your pet you will be the far greater sufferer.

When you have decided that there is no alternative to euthanasia, which, from the Greek, means "easy, painless death," then your dog will have to be brought to the vet for this final dispensation. Here again, should you or any members of the family wish to share in the final moments of your dog's life by being present, and perhaps holding him in your arms, then by all means tell the vet of your wishes. Very rarely will a vet refuse this poignant request from an owner. If he does, and it is that important to you, then your alternative is to find another vet. This issue is also best decided beforehand. If there are any problems with your vet obliging your request, your recourse is to make accomodations elsewhere. As with sitting at home until the final hour with your pet, if you are much too distraught to contain yourself and you suspect you will make an ugly scene at the vet, then lavish final embraces upon your dog, walk out of the vet's office, and don't turn back. Some people may be eternally tormented by the vision of a beloved dog lying dead in their arms. These people too should embrace the dog one final time, walk out of the vet's office, and remember their pal as he was in life, not in death. Whatever your choice, it is personal, and there are no recriminations forthcoming. Do what feels right in your heart, and your old dog will know you were with him till the very end.

If your dog dies in your home and in your arms, express your sorrow freely. Death bequeathes to the living the pain of loneliness and a terrible void.

Cremation

Before calling your vet, hopefully you will have decided whether you want the conventional option of cremation or some less ordinary choice. There are several.

It is conventional today to call the vet and have your dog taken from your home to the clinic, and then to a crematorium. This is the most common, and least expensive alternative. It does not oblige any formalized wake, as with humans, where the body is first embalmed and then placed on view for one to several days. Cremation is quick, simple, and inexpensive. Most people will opt for it, not only because of economy and practicality but because they have not stopped to consider other options. Most often, people aren't aware that other choices even exist. The vet will usually encourage his client toward the simple cremation procedures. He is thinking practically, not emotionally. But you must search your soul subjectively as well as rationally, to arrive at a meaningful decision for yourself, and for no one else. We do not make decisions such as these to please the neighbors, the vet, the in-laws, or the gregarious butcher who has long been a valued confidant to the family. If you feel in your heart that a less conventional disposal is in order for your dog, then by all means have the courage of your convictions, even in the face of some disconcerting ostracism by well-intentioned interlopers.

Cremation with subsequent interrment is done at the same place your vet would send all deceased dogs. However, if you have in mind either saving your dog's ashes in a special urn or casting his remains to the four winds in a spot of special significance to you, you will have to be prepared for extra cost. When crematoriums dispose of animals, it is done collectively. The fee to your vet, and subsequently the fee to you, is based on the volume- or multiple-disposal system. Should you decide to obtain your dog's remains, the crematorium will oblige you by accommodating your dog alone. The entire cost will be passed on to you, for operating costs remain the same for a single dog as for a group. If your inclination is strong in this direction, then try to arrange the details in advance with your vet as well as with the crematorium. If this is not done, you may find yourself undergoing something you do not want, simply because of the urgency of the matter. This truth holds for any of the less conventional means of disposal.

Home Burial

It was traditional for many years to dig a grave and bury your dog out in back of the barn, or in some lovely wooded sector of your property. In memorium, you would plant a tree or place some other monument above the place where he was interred. Most likely you would have hand-etched an epitaph over the spot where he was buried. Today we don't have so many burials in back of the barn or in a wooded glade, largely because most of us don't have a barn or a wooded glade to use. This was traditional and it was personal. It took some forethought, some physical effort, and a kind of responsibility that money can't buy. As traditionalists at heart, we find this option highly appealing and meaningful. You, of course, are limited in part by the availability of land for such purposes, and also by the respective health codes and laws of your town or city. If this option appeals to you, why not make a few phone calls and find out whether it would be feasible to inter your pet on your own home grounds. If not, you may possibly elect to use part of the grounds where your parents or in-laws live. You should take into account, however, the permanency of the abode. If you will be assuming eventual possession of the house, then it may be the ideal resting place for your beloved pet. If you live in an apartment in a big city, and have no plans for rural life now or in the future, this method of disposal may indeed be illogical for you.

Formal Burial

The last practical option is the commercial burial. Your dog is graced with much the same trappings that make up a human funeral. A casket is selected, the plot of ground is chosen, a suitable head stone is picked, an epitaph is inscribed, and your dog is interred in full regalia in a permanent resting place, together with many other beloved pets. Some of the monetary considerations would be—first—a plot. Plots range in size according to the size of the dog. Small ones sell for $150, whereas larger ones can cost $225 or more. Each plot can accomodate two pets and the ashes of a third. Next, you would select a burial container. Metal containers must be used and they cost about $30. If they are lined, the price escalates to $60. Should you desire a beautiful wood casket, the cost would range upwards from $120. However, the animal will still have to be buried in a metal container, so you can add the cost of the plain metal container at about $30, or the lined metal container at $60, to the price of the wooden casket.

There is a charge for opening and closing of the grave, which comes to approximately $30. If your dog is to be picked up, then a charge of $15 or more is added to the overall costs depending upon how far you live from the cemetary. On the selected grave plot you are entitled to a metal marker for one year. Thereafter you will pay a fee, unless you have selected a headstone. These can be obtained wherever they sell monuments for human graves, while some pet cemetaries have sample monuments on view for selection. Monuments can cost upwards of $100, and if your tastes are elaborate they could cost $1000 or more. There is a one-dollar-per-letter charge for the inscription on a headstone. If you elected to place a metal marker on the gravesight for the first year, taking time to select a suitable headstone, then the inscription fee would be charged a second time for the new permanent headstone. Pet cemetaries charge about $5 as an annual maintenance fee; perpetual maintenance can be had for about $200. In the area of optional services, you may elect a Christmas decoration at an annual charge of $5, or Special Care (including seasonal flowers and Christmas decorations) at $15 annually. You may also elect to have Perpetual Special Care at a cost of approximately $500.

We have covered most of the items involved in a formalized burial for your dog. As you can see, this is the most expensive option, with a total cost ranging from $200 on upward. But it may be the right choice for you. No one but you can decide how special your dog was to you. If you are one of those people who view your animal as another person, then perhaps it will be most fitting for you to immortalize him in much the same way you would a person.

A commercial burial for a pet is different than for humans in a few ways. The pet is laid out in a casket without embalming. Since there is no three-day wake, it is not necessary to preserve the body chemically against deterioration. Also, as far as we know, there are no provisions for funeral services. You may be able to arrange a special service for your pet with your pastor or minister, but it is not part of the functions of the normal commercial pet burial. There is, however, a small viewing room where your pet can be placed in an open casket, and anyone wishing to may pay his last respects. There are a number of pets laid out in this viewing room at the same time, perhaps eight or ten, and viewing time is a matter of hours rather than days.

It is not mercenary to consider in advance all the options open to you in respect to the eventuality of your dog's death. Most books dealing with the subject of pets and death circumvent the basic psychological and economic questions as being too indelicate for pursuit. To do that is to deny the existence of death as a solid reality. If you have read this far, you are undoubtedly possessed of loving, rational concern for your pet. Any path you choose, in loving memorium to your dog, will be the right choice because it is right for you.

In loving memorium to his own dog, the poet Lord Byron wrote:

Near this spot lie the remains of one who possessed Beauty
without Vanity,
Strength without Insolence,
Courage without Ferocity,
and all the virtues of Man without his vices.

This praise, which would be unmeaning flattery if inscribed over human ashes, is but a just tribute to the memory of Boatswain—a Dog

Chapter IX

THE BEGINNING FOLLOWS THE END: THE NEW PUPPY

Housebreaking Routine

Now that you have a new little puppy in your household, you will want to start him on the road to civility as soon as possible. To do this, it is necessary to realize some of the temporary problems you will meet. Your puppy has been in an environment where he was not required to discipline his excretory habits. When mother nature called, your puppy happily answered. This is fine, up to a point. Your new puppy is rapidly developing a mind, so that he can now be expected to adhere to a program of limited responsibility. Should you allow your puppy to indescriminately soil your floors with his excrement, you will find yourself down on all fours almost as constantly as he is. Housebreaking is the number one bugaboo when bringing a new pup into a household, but it needn't be a problem. All you require is the knowledge and a few necessary tools to make housebreaking happen for you and your pet in some one to two weeks.

All obedience problems are basically a question of faulty communication between you and your pet. This is not his fault because, for the most part, he would be overjoyed to cooperate with you if only you had a clear and concise way of conveying your requirements to him. I say *requirements* and not wishes for a very good reason. You are going to begin setting down guidelines for your pet to follow, and you will introduce your requirements very slowly, clearly, and patiently. He, likewise, should have an opportunity to absorb these instructions in a very calm, unharassed manner. Losing your cool, or

129

The beginning follows the end: The new puppy.

displaying irrational frustration over mistakes made on the floor, does neither of you any good. Your dog reacts in perplexity, and therein lies the seeds for blossoming neurosis. It is certainly difficult to act rationally all the time in a highly irrational world, but, as we have assumed a great responsibility—as with childrearing too—we must attempt to do the best we can in the given circumstances.

For housebreaking you will need a chain collar (about two inches larger than his neck, for comfortable fit); a six-foot web leash, for taking him on those all-important walks outside; a three-to-four-foot piece of clothesline (which your pup will drag behind him in the house when you are around to watch him); a bolt snap, purchasable in any hardware store, to which clothesline will be attached, and which then snaps to the collar; and a bottle of liquid Nilodor to deodorize the area where mistakes do occur. Nilodor is used because it completely removes the scent of urine and fecal matter, making it impossible for the dog to relocate the site of his error and thereby be tempted to repeat it. Dogs identify strongly with the scent of excrement. They love to make either where they have gone before or where another dog has gone whose scent they wish to overcome and replace. This is a sort of territorial imperative; a canine calling card, if you will. Bleaches and commercial cleaners do not have the power to negate the smell that attracts that all-too-powerful nose. A dog's sense of smell is about seven times as acute as our own. But then, thankfully, we are not impelled to obscure someone else's excrement with our own. We have spiritual, psychological, biological, and many other rationales for our being. But a dog, unable to intellectualize, sees his excrement as an empirical rationale of his existence.

Next you must locate an area for the confinement of your dog, both for overnight and for the times when you can't be with him, such as shopping, visiting a neighbor, etc. For the confinement, we suggest the kitchen as being most suitable, since it has a tile surface that is hard and cold and is less apt to absorb odors. It can also be wiped up easily should any mistakes occur. The mechanism to be used for confinement is a simple expanding gate, the kind used to block off doorways or stairways for the safety of youngsters. We do not use cages because you will be enlarging the area gradually and you cannot enlarge a cage. You will have to find a corner, perhaps between two appliances or an appliance and the wall, to set off a box or rectangle only a little larger than the dog's own size. The reason for this is that dogs don't like to make where they sleep, and if they would be forced to lie in excrement they will choose to hold it in.

Gate enclosure for confining the puppy overnight or when you are out. The same type of gate is used for paper-training and housebreaking.

Should you confine your dog in a space too large, where he can make in one spot and lie in another, then that is exactly what he will do. Miscalculation on your part, which would lead to such opportunity for your dog, would only make housebreaking that much more confusing to the pup and harder for you.

Here you have the whole picture as far as equipment is concerned: a chain collar, a six-foot web leash, a bolt snap, a three-foot piece of clothesline, a bottle of liquid Nilodor, and an expandable gate to be used in front of the area of confinement.

Of equally great importance is giving your dog the proper diet. Canned meat mixed with a dry cereal or meal is the simplest thing to feed a puppy you are going to housebreak. If the dog were to be fed dehydrated packaged burgers or all dry, packaged, dehydrated foods, he would tend to drink more water and thereby urinate more frequently, making housebreaking very difficult. (See the diet chart at the end of this chapter for the correct ration of meat to meal, according to size and age.)

The next important aspect in housebreaking is to properly follow the food and walk schedule as your guideline, and stick to it as closely as possible. We mention on the schedule that food and water are to be left down only ten minutes. This is to control more closely your dog's understanding that when food is put down, it is to be eaten then. You will not be able to calculate when your dog has to make if you don't know exactly when he ate. For the purposes of housebreaking only, you will also remove the water after ten minutes.

After your dog is housebroken, he will be able to control himself and water can be left down for him to drink at his discretion.

Puppies eat three or four times a day (see schedule); older dogs eat twice. All dogs eat at least twice a day. It is too much of a load on the digestive organs to eat the complete nutritional requirements in one meal. Following the diet chart, if your puppy is less than three months of age, you will be feeding him four times a day; and from three to six months old, three times a day. Try to make the last meal at the 3:30 feeding. In this way your dog will have a full six hours plus before his last walk, as it takes approximately four to six hours for a dog to process his food. When he makes after that time, you will be assured of an empty dog and a comfortable dog throughout the night. Should you be a working individual or couple, try to feed the puppy as soon as you get home, and then take him out for his last walk just before you go to bed. Always empty the dog the first thing in the morning, before he eats, and, if you are a working couple, the first thing when you return home after work, before he has supper. We should mention that, realistically, housebreaking will take a little longer if you are a working couple, because you will not be around to catch his every mistake. Your pup cannot be confined to a small gated area all night *and all day as well!* So, you will have to compromise and leave the pup in a more open kitchen area, with water down during the day, especially in the hot summer. Leave no newspapers down unless you are trying to paper train him, which is a seperate procedure altogether. Simply wipe up any mistakes that occur during the day, *say nothing*, and continue with your schedule as described.

After your ten-minute food and water periods, you should then take the dog for a five-to-ten-minute walk. The timing here is also very important, since longer walks will obscure for him the reason he is being walked. (Later on, when your pup is housebroken, the ten-minute walk limit will no longer apply.) You should take your pup out for walks on the six-foot web leash, and the chain collar should be left on at all times since it must be of the proper fit. Should the collar be too big, with you hoping he will grow into it, your dog may slip out of the collar and run out into traffic. If after ten minutes your dog has not excreted his wastes, take him back inside and exchange the web leash for the short clothesline with the bolt snap. Allow your dog to run free in the same room where you are working or relaxing, and *watch him*. Should he start to make on the floor, yell NO loudly, and quickly grab the clothesline and drag him outside to finish his mak-

Puppy installation of chain collar. Form the letter "P".

ing. This procedure is called "catching the dog in the act." His "act" will never be exhibited on the centerfold of *Playgirl*, but the more responsive you are in catching him making, the quicker he will be hustled to the door without any mistakes.

As soon as he finishes making, give your dog some praise, saying, GOOD BOY. This is the very necessary contrast between correction, NO, and praise, GOOD BOY, that will begin to clarify for your dog what is expected of him and where. He will also look forward to the praise and become more eager to please you. In "catching him in the act," there is no time to change from the clothesline to the leash. The reason he drags the line is so you will have a quick way of hustling him outside to finish his business. The leash is used on the scheduled walks and the clothesline is for mistakes in transit. Do not worry if most of the excrement landed on your kitchen floor, or dribbled down the front steps or walkway. The important thing is that your dog is learning: *He cannot make in the house and get away with it.* When you both come back inside, just Nilodor (15 drops to 3 cups of water) the mistake and continue about your regular activities. Do not use the "rub his nose in it" routine, or yell and scream obscenities, or rattle or throw a can so that your pup will develop an early fear of loud noises. Yell NO only once, loudly and firmly, and

Ralphie Boy and Opieline sit and stay at attention, awaiting their next command.

by all means don't forget the GOOD BOY once he has finished outside, even if there was only a drop left to squeeze out.

When you must leave your pup for an hour or two, and when you retire, place him in the gate confinement. Remember to have the confinement not much larger than the dog's size, or else he will make in one corner and lie down in another. For much longer intervals, confinement will have to be half of the kitchen or even the whole kitchen. If the family can cooperate for one to two weeks of concentrated effort, you will find housebreaking accomplished in a minimum of time and with a minimum of mishaps.

You may wish to paper-train your dog as an alternative to housebreaking. If you have a small-breed dog, are an elderly couple, a handicapped person, or have many stairs to contend with, you may choose paper-training as a permanent alternative to housebreaking. In paper-training your dog, the food, water, and walk schedule is the same, but this time your dog should be placed on the papers. You should use either the bathroom or any room of your choice. Completely cover the entire area with newspapers. When your dog makes, praise him, GOOD BOY, and then watch him with the line dragging. Each day you should remove a few more newspapers, retaining one of the papers already scented with urine to place on top of the new batch. This will enable him to find his scent more easily and become paper-trained more quickly. Each day less and less of the floor area should be covered with papers, until you find your dog eliminating in one small area of the room. Your dog should be confined at night in this room with the papers. Nilodor should be used to deodorize any mistakes off the paper. Essentially, you will be able to housebreak or paper-train your pet within two weeks if these instructions are followed closely.

Karen has learned to carry Fluffy with proper support.

DIET CHART

AGE	SIZE OF DOG	MEAL	MEAT (CANNED)
Weaning to 3 months	Small breeds	¼ cup	¼-½ can
	Medium breeds	⅓ cup	½ can
4 meals a day	Large breeds	½ cup	½-¾ can
	Very large breeds	½-¾ cup	¾ can
3 to 6 months	Small breeds	½ cup	½-¾ can
	Medium breeds	¾ cup	¾ can
3 meals a day	Large breeds	¾ cup	1 can
	Very large breeds	1 ½ cups	1-1 ¾ can
over 6 months	Small breeds	½ cup	½-¾ can
	Medium breeds	¾-1 cup	¾-1 ¼ cans
2 meals a day	Large breeds	2 cups	1 ½-2 ½ cans
	Very large breeds	2-4 cups	2 ¼-5 cans

THE SCHEDULE

Feedings and Walks, 3 months old eating 3 times a day. Food left down 10 minutes only.

7:55 First thing in the morning, fast walk to urinate.
8:00 Food and Water
8:10 Walk (5 to 10 minutes on leash only to make)
11:30 Food and Water
11:40 Walk
3:30 Food and Water (Last solid food of the day)
3:40 Walk
7:00 Water and Walk
9:30 Water and Walk
11:30 Walk (no water)

FREQUENTLY ASKED QUESTIONS CONCERNING THE OLDER DOG

Q. Do dogs have to go out for walks more often as they get older?

A. Yes, but for different reasons. If we are dealing with a normal, healthy dog, he can get along on the frequency he is used to. However, if you have an older dog that is beginning to show arthritis problems, it is a good idea to get him moving more often during the day. The older dog can also tend to get lazy, and circulation is improved with moderate walks.

Q. Is a dog's bladder weaker at eight or nine years old?

A. Most of the time, what is interpreted as a weak bladder is actually a bladder infection or an ensuing kidney problem. Bladder infections can be common, regardless of age, and kidney disease is very pronounced in the older dog. Two of the most common problems in the older dog are bad heart and bad kidneys.

Q. If the older dog begins to urinate in the house for apparently no reason, after being housebroken for many years, would you assume this to be a medical problem rather than spite-work?

A. Yes, most definitely. You must first eliminate any medical problems before you chastise your dog for disobedience. Medically speaking, if he is urinating in the house, this is most likely a bladder problem. If he is drinking more water and also urinating in the house, it could more likely be a kidney problem.

Q. Is exercise bad for the older dog?

A. No. Exercise is very good for a dog unless there are definite contraindications, such as heart problems. All exercise should be within reason. Jumping hurdles is exercise that the older dog should not be asked to do, but walking provides healthful exercise for all dogs of any age.

Q. Do older dogs need a different diet?

139

A. Yes. They should have less total protein but a higher-quality protein. Different age dogs do require different diets. Young dogs need a high concentration of protein, middle-aged dogs can thrive on the protein that exists in the average good-quality dog food, and older dogs need lesser amounts of higher-quality protein. Excess protein produces more nitrogenous wastes, which means more work for the kidneys. Dogs with kidney problems could be put on prescription dog food, or small amounts of high-quality protein, such as in eggs, yogurt, tofu, ricotta, farmer cheese, cottage cheese, and hard mild cheeses, together with a lot of raw, grated vegetables. Kidney problems require low protein. Heart problems require low salt. Very often the two maladies go hand in hand.

Q. Do older dogs lose their teeth as do humans?

A. Yes, but for slightly different reasons. Excessive tartar builds up. This creates a bacterial climate whereby destructive agents invade the gum and bone surfaces, causing damage or destruction to both, and eventual tooth loss in some dogs. Machines such as the cavitron have been used with some success in removing excess tartar from a dog's teeth. Once the dog has bitten down on a piece of food, the outer surfaces are not utilized very much so most of the tartar forms on the outside of the teeth. The inner surfaces are being stimulated more by the action of chewing and therefore remain cleaner.

Q. Why do dogs live such a relatively short life span?

A. Every type of animal has a predetermined life span and we cannot deduce any logical or medical rationales for the relatively short life span of dogs. However, all dogs will reach their maximum longevity if kept in good health. A proper diet will increase your dog's lifespan.

Q. Why do small dogs live relatively longer than the larger breeds?

A. It probably has something to do with the metabolic rate. The greatest difference occurs within the very large breeds, such as the St. Bernards, Great Danes, Irish Wolfhounds. Their average life span might be eight or nine years, as opposed to a tiny Poodle or Chihuahua that can seemingly live on forever, becoming senior citizens of eighteen or nineteen years old.

Q. What is the most humane way of ending a dog's life?

A. Euthanasia, as performed by an overdose of anesthesia, is the most painless way of ending a dog's life. He simply goes to sleep, in a matter of seconds, and feels no pain or apprehension. Phenobarbital is the anesthesia used. Some facilities use suffocation, which means putting the dog in an evacuation chamber and extracting the air, a method most often employed where cost dictates mass disposal. This procedure, of course, is much less humane and to be avoided wherever possible. Carbon monoxide is also used, and could be considered a second alternative to the phenobarbital.

Q. How often should the older dog be bathed?

A. The older dog, as well as any age dog, should be bathed whenever he is dirty, and as often as he needs it, in a mild, natural, herbal shampoo from a health food store.

Q. Do older dogs need special vitamins?

A. An older dog should be on a good multivitamin, mineral, trace mineral, intestinal flora, and enzyme preparation, because he does not absorb nutrients as well from the intestinal tract.

Q. Is the surgical risk greater in the older dog?

A. Usually yes, again depending upon the status of the heart and the kidneys. All of this should be thoroughly checked out before the older dog is anesthetised. The anesthesia provides a greater risk than the surgery. If the dog is competently evaluated before surgery, there should only be a one-percent risk factor of anesthetic death. During the time when sodium pentobarbital was more widely used for anesthesia, many dogs never woke up because of a condition called acidosis. Overdosing caused excess absorption of the pentobarbital into the body. Just when you would think the dog was nicely asleep, his fat began to release it, thereby effecting an overdose in the dog. When sodium pentobarbital is in the blood stream, there is no control or reversal. Today, with gas anesthesia, risk is almost nil because of the greater control the vet has.

Q. Do dogs get arthritis as they get older?

A. Some do. Larger dogs are more prone to arthritis because of hip dysplasia, and because of the proclivity to hip dysplasia, they also get arthritis in the hip joints. But dogs don't have to be old to get arthritis. Small dogs are less prone to arthritis, regardless of their age. The general correlation does not preclude the existence of one condition without the other; however, the two usually do go together.

Q. Do older dogs need more sleep?

A. They probably rest more, but this indicates a lessening of physical activity rather than excessive sleeping.

Q. Do older dogs eat less?

A Growing dogs eat twice as much as those no longer growing, but, once they attain adulthood, they generally stabilize their eating habits. However, a sick dog, no matter what his age, will generally

141

stop eating altogether. Older dogs will tend to eat less.

Q. Can an older dog be hurt by using a metal choke chain to train him, or even just to walk him?

A. Metal chain collars are prefectly safe as long as the dog is in good physical condition. Nylon choke collars provide an alternative.

Q. How often do dogs get heart attacks?

A. Dogs don't get heart attacks as they manifest themselves in humans. If a dog gets a heart block, related to an arterial obstruction, he can drop dead but it wouldn't be a heart attack. However, dogs do get strokes, which would indicate an obstruction leading to the brain. Heart attack is not a veterinary term.

Q. What is the most common cause of death in dogs?

A. Cars kill more dogs than all other causes combined, more than all diseases. Irresponsible dog owners are the real killers, the cars are merely the means of execution. Among diseases, kidney and heart diseases take equal toll, and cancer is a more common cause of death nowadays than heretofore.

Let us repeat here what was stated earlier. There must be respect for community leash laws. Dogs should not walk themselves. Always *take your dog for his walks*, whether to answer a call of nature or just for a stroll, *on the leash*. We, the dog owners, have that responsibility to our pets; their safety and longevity depend on us.

Q. What can be done for a very old dog with severe dysplasia problems?

A. First, the condition would have to be evaluated through x rays. The symptoms may be due to a neurological problem and not a bone problem. If surgery is indicated, and the dog is checked out as a good surgical risk, operating can prove very helpful in alleviating the pain. Excellent results have also been obtained using vitamin C therapy. (See the section on *Hip Dysplasia* in Chapter IV.)

Q. What is the incidence of cancer in dogs?

A. Cancer incidence is low as compared with humans. Even when there exists a lipoma, a benign fatty tumor, or breast tumors that are diagnosed as malignant, these do not precipitate a spreading malignancy or death. Occasionally dogs will have a liver or spleen tumor that spreads to the lungs. Such dogs can bleed to death because the tumors bleed, or the malignancy can cause sufficient damage to the liver to cause death. Fibrosis of the heart and kidneys, which means a loss of elasticity in those organs, is far and away the most common disease-induced cause of death. Cancer affects more cats than dogs, but the reasons for this are somewhat obscure. Much can be done to control and prevent cancer in dogs. (See the sections on *Cancer* and *Breast Tumors* in Chapter IV.)

Q. Is the older dog more affected by heat prostration?

A. Yes, an older dog's thermostat does not work as well, so he will be more affected by extremes of heat and cold. If a dog has a bad heart or bad kidneys, he will be more affected than the healthier dog. However, if you were to put a two-year-old dog and an eleven-year-old, both in good physical condition, into a sun-baked car, they will both suffer with equal severity and trauma.

Q. Is it advantageous for an older dog to wear protective clothing of any kind?

A. Wearing apparel we would define as being generally superfluous. However, there are some good reasons for wearing clothing on certain occasions. (See the section on *Clothing* in Chapter III.)

Q. Are older dogs subject to high blood pressure?

A. If a dog has a bad heart, he usually has low blood pressure because he is hampered by an inefficient pump and poor circulation. This is why a dog with heart problems often also has kidney problems. You must maintain adequate pressure and blood supply to organs in order to maximize kidney efficiency.

Q. Should an owner take his own dog's temperature?

A. No! In consideration of safety factors such as thermometer breakage and absorbing the thermometer up into the rectum, as well as not being able to diagnose the symptoms concurrent to the temperature (which at 101° to 102° is normal in a dog), we advise people not to take their own dog's temperature, but to call the vet without delay if they suspect illness.

Q. How old should a male dog be before he should be prevented from copulating?

A. Dogs generally have a self-checking mechanism, which means that they would not ordinarily pursue sex beyond their abilities and fortitude. If they did attempt copulation beyond their physical stamina, they would simply pass out. As dogs get older, they have a lower sperm count, so for selective breeding purposes you are better off using a younger dog with not only fine conformation but stable temperament as well. (Refer to *How to Train Your Dog in Six Weeks* to find out how to select for temperament.)

Q. How old should a bitch be when weaning her last litter?

A. In general, a female should not be more than five years old when weaning her last litter, nor younger than the second heat, which means between one and two years old. She should also be

143

bred only every other heat, which means a total of three or four litters throughout a female's lifetime.

Q. Do female dogs experience a change of life?

A. Not that we are aware of. Female dogs can remain fertile until they die. We know of a cocker spaniel who had puppies at the age of fourteen. For the most part bitches simply stop coming into heat, or come into heat less often, without any menopausal symptoms such as hot flashes, etc.

Q. What is the oldest a dog can live?

A. We have heard of dogs living to eighteen years. In general, these cases occur among the smaller breeds.

Q. How does a dog's hearing or sight change as he gets older?

A. It generally gets worse. Barring any medical problems, it is not uncommon to see normal longevity of nine to fifteen years in a dog that has become deaf. The older dog will lose his hearing gradually, so that his owner is often not aware of it until the dog is deaf or almost deaf. Dogs very rarely become blind, but many will experience a clouding of the lens as they get older. A dog's sight is comprised of rods but no cones, so they don't see color—only shades of black, white, and gray.

Q. Do older dogs tend to get fat?

A. Dogs in general tend to be overfed. They are being killed with kindness through frequent snacking. However, older dogs, like people, will tend to loose muscle tone. Overfeeding and lack of exercise will cause any age dog to become overweight.

Q. How common is the problem of gastric torsion?

A. It seems to occur primarily in big dogs. The condition usually is precipitated by a heavy, fatty meal, eaten hastily, followed closely by a lot of water then by exercise. The stomach is contracting, trying to digest food and building up fermentation momentum until, in the big-chested dog, the stomach literally flips over, twists, and closes off the openings at both ends. It can be remedied only by immediate surgery to unflip the stomach and sew it to the stomach wall if necessary. If not caught in time, the dog goes into shock and dies.

Q. Can older dogs develop cataracts?

A. Yes, but cataracts can also be seen in younger dogs.

Q. Do mixed breeds live longer than pure breeds?

A. We don't find that the longevity differs greatly between mixed and purebred dogs.

Q. Are there any kinds of parasites that would particularly affect older dogs?

A. If an older dog gets hookworms, it might affect him more. In general, it all depends upon the dog's state of well-being.

Q. Are organ transplants performed in older dogs?

A. These operations are performed experimentally. But practically, the cost would be prohibitive, not to mention the problem of availability of organs.

Q. Do older dogs shed more?

A. No, they may even shed less. But they may develop more seborrhea.

Q. What dog diseases are communicable to humans?

A. Ringworm, rabies, sarcoptic mange, ticks, can all be communicated to humans. Incidentally, ringworm is a fungus disease of the skin and, as such, it is a misnomer. In the case of sarcoptic mange, when you kill it on the dog, the human symptoms will disappear.

Q. Does an aging dog become senile?

A. In general, no, unless there are other circumstances involved, such as a brain tumor.

Q. Do dogs utilize their full capacity of intelligence?

A. We know, and most people are amazed to discover, that a dog has a tremendous capacity for learning, regardless of age. This potential is seldom tapped by most dog owners.

Q. Are there special food considerations for diabetic dogs?

A. Yes. In general, you should not be using the semimoist packaged foods for a diabetic dog, because of the sugar they contain that moderate in whole grains, and high in high-biological-value dairy products.

Q. Can you tell a dog's age by the condition of its teeth?

A. No. Some two-year-old dogs could chew on rocks and have teeth that look like the dog is fifteen. Others retain the shape and color through very advanced years.

Q. Is there any age beyond which you should not purchase a dog?

A. You should try to find out why the dog is being sold at an advanced age. If he is aggressive, you likely will have a problem. But if you are satisfied that the reasons are valid as to why the dog is being given up, then, beyond the fact that you will have a shorter life together, the love that passes between you will be just as strong and meaningful as if it had been a complete life span.

Q. Is there any special training equipment that should be used for the older dog?

145

A. No. The chain collar and six-foot web leash are applicable for all training sessions with a normal healthy dog, regardless of age.

Q. Why don't dogs get cavities except in rare instances?

A. It is speculated that the enamel surface of the dog's teeth is harder and more impenetrable to pathogenisis than that of humans. Another factor could be that the dog is presumed to not to have amylase in the saliva as humans do; so, while human starch-digestion begins in the mouth, the dog's starch-digestion starts further down the intestinal tract. Some research has since discovered salivary enzymes.

Q. Which breeds tend to have the greatest incidence of pyorrhea (bone degeneration), leading to loss of teeth?

A. The two breeds we find with the most frequent incidence of periodontal disease are the Dachshunds and Schnauzers. The host resistance factor seems to be lower in these breeds.

Q. How septic is a dog's mouth?

A. Since bacteria do not break through the body's protective barrier, namely the skin, we needn't worry about having a dog lick us and our subsequently contracting a disease. However, from the point of aesthetics, dogs do sniff every conceivable pile or puddle of excrement deposited in the streets by other dogs, so many people may deem it ill-advised to allow a dog to lick them on the mouth. This choice is entirely personal. The people who sleep with their dogs usually allow all manner of familiarity, including kissing.

Q. What are ear hematomas and what causes them?

A. Usually a hematoma is precipitated by irritation of some sort within the ear or upon the ear flap. The dog tries to ease the annoyance by shaking his head, frequently hitting his ears against solid objects and rupturing the veins of the ears. This causes internal bleeding, which collects in a swelling beneath the skin until the blood clots. Hematomas can resorb, but the dog winds up with a cauliflower ear. The surgery performed for ear hematomas is cosmetic, not crucial to the dog's health.

Q. How does one dog react to the death of another dog in the family?

A. This can be very personally traumatic for a dog. Just as some dogs will refuse to eat, and subsequently will starve to death, after the death of their master, the emotional affinity can be exceedingly strong between one family pet and another.

Q. Should a new puppy be introduced into a family with the older dog?

A. We advise against this for several reasons. The older dog may bully the younger pup, causing permanent damage to the pup's personality. Also, the older dog may feel forced to compete, resenting strongly the presence of this newcomer. An older dog, in resentment, may try to hurt, or even kill, the new puppy, causing a tragedy that you can well live without. Sometimes the older dog gets a more acute awareness of his age and debilities, causing him undue stress and unhappiness. On the plus side, some older dogs have been known to become rejuvenated by a new canine family member. A sedate older dog can sometimes act as a calming influence upon a young boisterous puppy. Chewing and barking problems are sometimes lessened when anxiety is diminished through companionship. But, here again, it is just as possible for a new dog to pick up bad habits from an older dog, as it is likely that he will pick up the good habits. We advise that you do both yourself and your dog a service by not introducing a new puppy into the family until such time as your present devoted companion has died. At that time, we advise wholeheartedly, go out and purchase another dog!

Appendix

LIST OF HEALTH SUPPLIERS
AND SERVICES

Aloe Vera Products, Inc.
2644 North Ashland Avenue
Chicago, IL 60614
Tel: 312-871-7552

Leading grower of aloe vera products: ointments, gel, juices, shampoos, soaps, live plants, and scrubs.

American Academy of Medical Preventics
305 South Doheny Drive
Beverly Hills, CA 90211
Tel: 213-878-1234

Nonprofit educational referral society for health care professionals.

Aphrodesia Herbal Products, Inc.
45 Washington Street
Brooklyn, NY 11201
Tel: 212-852-1278

Herbs, potpourri, botanicals, fragrance, essential oils, Edgar Cayce products, teas, gelatin capsules, books.

Aquarian Fish Products (By Mardel Labs)
714 North Yale Avenue
Villa Park, IL 60181

High quality fish foods, new health products for birds, "Ornibac" (an acidophilus culture for stress).

Arizona Natural Products, Inc.
7750 East Evans Road
Suite #3
Scottsdale, AZ 85260
Tel: 602-991-4414

Manufactures whole clove odorless garlic, yeast, bee pollen, and lecithin.

Arrowhead Mills, Inc. (Deaf Smith Country)
P.O. Box 866
Hereford, TX 79045
Tel: 806-364-0730

One of the largest processors of natural whole grains, unrefined vegetable and seed oils, "talking food brochures," beans, seeds, nuts, fruit and nut butters, cereals, baking mixes, whole grain flours. Write for information on whole foods and processing.

Aubrey Organics
4419 North Manhattan Avenue
Tampa, FL 33614
Tel: 813-877-4186

Very high quality line natural cosmetics, herbal rinses, jojoba oil, therapeutic shampoos, loofa, and skin lotions. Never tests on animals.

Bio-Zyme Enterprises, Inc.
P.O. Box 428
1231 Alabama
St. Joseph, MO 64504
Tel: 816-238-3326

Nutritional enzyme supplements for horses, dogs, and cats.

Boerke and Tafel, Inc.
1011 Arch Street
Philadelphia, PA 19107
Tel: 215-922-2967

Homeopathic preparations, schuesslers cell salts, tinctures, cod liver oil tablets, witch hazel.

Borden, Inc. (Pet Ag division, Pet/Vet Products)
RR 1 Box 127
Elgin, IL 60120
Tel: 312-741-3131

Milk replacers for orphaned animals, esbilac, KRM, SPF-LAC, Foal-LAC. These formulas can be used to raise young of other exotic species.

Borneman and Sons, Inc.
1208 Amosland Road
P.O. Box 54
Norwood, PA 19074
Tel: 215-532-2035

Books, homeopathic preparations, cell salts, ointments, tinctures.

Branstone Bakery
25 J Commercial Boulevard
Novato, CA 94947

Natural dog biscuits.

Cher Ami Natural Pet Foods, Inc.
34-01 38th Avenue
Long Island City, NY 11101
Tel: 212-729-4306

Sweet Treat dog biscuits, petit cheese, Le Cheez dog biscuits. Some of the finest products of this type.

Doris Day Pet Foundation
P.O. Box 600
Beverly Hills, CA 90213

Medical assistance programs, food, lodging, adoption service, lost and found, foster homes, requests donations to help homeless animals.

Duro Test Corporation International
2321 Kennedy Boulevard
North Bergen, NJ 07047
Tel: 201-867-7000

Vita-Lite, natural full spectrum for plants, animals, and people.

Eden Ranch, Organic Consumer Report
Gwenith Lee Morales
P.O. Box 370
Topanga, CA 90290
Tel: 213-455-1336

Interesting and informative capsulated data on health and nutrition.

Foods of Nature Pet Food
P.O. Box 1515
Covina, CA 91722
Tel: 213-332-1016

Good quality natural pet foods, supplements, health products for birds, shampoos, herbal wormers, herbal flea collars.

Herbal Animal Natural Pet Care Products
P.O. Box 8702
Oakland, CA 94662

Herbal wormers, supplements, flea collars, insect repellants.

Hippocrates Health Institute
Dr. Ann Wigmore
25 Exeter Street
Boston, MA 02116
Tel: 607-267-9525

Wheatgrass, sprouts, raw food therapy for people and pets, books, courses, lectures, detoxification programs.

Lightning Products
11636 54th Street North
Clearwater, FL 33520
Tel: 813-577-5643

Environmental protection pet products for dogs, cats, and horses; shampoos, skin treatment, cleansers.

Luyties Pharmacal Company
4200 Laclede Avenue
St. Louis, MO 63108
Tel: 314-533-9600

Homeopathic preparations, cell salts, books, vitamins, ointments.

McHugh Animal Nutritionists
866 Independence Avenue
Mt. View, CA 94043
Tel: 415-967-8815

High quality line of food supplements for dogs, cats, birds, and other pets; Ultra-mend, Ultra-glo, Ultra-scorbate.

National Enzyme Company
6215 West Belmont Avenue
Chicago, IL 60634
Tel: 312-622-6662

Fine quality digestive enzymes.

Natural Hygiene Society, Inc.
698 Brooklawn Avenue
Bridgeport, CT 06604
Tel: 203-366-6229

Dedicated to science of health; books, information, *Health Science* magazine.

Nil'Odor, Inc. (Concentrated deodorizing products)
7740 Freedom Avenue, NW
P.O. Box 2349
North Canton, OH 44720
Tel: 216-499-4321

Excellent odor neutralizer and housebreaking aid, nontoxic.

Natures Gate Health and Beauty Products
9740 Cozycroft Avenue
Chatsworth, CA 91311
Tel: 213-882-2951

Pet shampoos with natural flea repellants.

Natural Animal
699 Taraval Street
San Francisco, CA 94116

Jojoba products for dogs and cats.

Pines Wheatgrass International
P.O. Box 357
Hays, KS 67601
Tel: 913-628-3076

Manufactures high-quality wheatgrass in powder, capsule, and pellet form for dogs, cats, people, and all small animals.

Prevention Magazine
Emmaus, PA 18049
Tel: 215-967-5171

Well-known, informative publication on matters of health and nutrition.

Solid Gold Health Products for Pets
P.O. Box 2341
9490 Loren Drive
La Mesa, CA 92041
Tel: 619-465-9507

Herbal dog food, natural biscuits, yeast, skin cream, natural wormers, herbal flea collars, vitamin C scorbate, shampoos, repellents, heartworm detection kits, tick tongs.

Vital Nutrition Products, Inc.
25 Laurel Road
Rocky Hill, CT 06067
Tel: 203-721-8422

Food supplements for dogs and cats, flea fighter formula.

Westward Products
P.O. Box 1032
12021 Ventura Place
Studio City, CA 91604
Tel: 213-761-1112

Herb-etts, Kleen Air, shampoos, worm-etts, anti-itch pet lotion. Well-established company supplying fine quality herbal products for dogs, cats, and horses.

—FOR NUTRITIONAL COUNSELING—

Kathy Berman's Eubiotics Ltd.
90 New York Avenue
West Hempstead, NY 11552
Tel: 516-485-9252

—FOR DOG TRAINING—

Bill Landesman's Happy Tails Dog Training Academy
7 Rudolph Drive
Carle Place, NY 11514
Tel: 516-741-5869

Dog training in the home, housebreaking, obedience, guard work

EPILOGUE

When all you have is gone,
and all who love you have left,
he still remains faithful.
His loyalty reaches even beyond the barrier of time.
His affection and respect cannot be bought,
but must be earned;
he cannot be bribed by food
as can all other animals,
proving their inferiority to him.
You are everything to him—
his life centers around you;
your praise is his greatest gift,
your scorn his deepest sorrow.
Ready to serve you at any time,
he is only too eager and willing to prove it:
glad to defend you against any odds,
he will give his life for yours
without your ever asking.
He would jump willingly into the fires of hell
just to be there with you.
Ready, he stands at your side
like his ancestors have done before him
and his offspring will do after him.
Whether gently playing with your children
or guarding your mate with his life,
he does his job well
with an understanding almost superhuman.
He has only one fault,
and that is—someday
he will break your heart.
For dogs live only a little while,
and in a few quick years
he must say goodbye.

                    Bill Landesman